The New York Times

OBAMA

THE HISTORIC JOURNEY

Senator Barack Obama at a rally in Rodney Square, Wilmington, Del. February 3, 2008.

DAMON WINTER/NYT

The candidate speaking in a heavy rain at a rally, Widener University, Chester, Pa. October 28, 2008.

DAMON WINTER/NYT

*Campaigning in Orlando, Fla., with Senator Hillary Rodham Clinton,
Obama's one-time opponent. October 20, 2008.*

*President-elect Barack Obama and his running mate,
Vice President-elect Joseph R. Biden Jr. of Delaware,
with their wives, Michelle Obama and Jill Biden,
at an election night rally in Grant Park, Chicago.
November 4, 2008.*

A woman in Grant Park, Chicago, yells, "Thank you, God!" as CNN announces that Senator Obama will become the next president of the United States. November 4, 2008.

Senator Barack Obama speaks at a campaign rally in Pueblo, Colo. November 1, 2008.

DAMON WINTER/NYT

The New York Times

OBAMA
THE HISTORIC JOURNEY

INTRODUCTION BY BILL KELLER
BIOGRAPHICAL TEXT BY JILL ABRAMSON

EDITORS
VINCENT ALABISO, NICHOLAS CALLAWAY, AMY CLOUD,
CATHY FERRARA, NANCY LEE, ALEX WARD

ART DIRECTOR
TOSHIYA MASUDA

The New York Times

CALLAWAY

NEW YORK
2009

CONTENTS

DOUG MILLS/NYT

Senator Obama and his family walk near a cornfield in Kempton, Ind., where they went to a potluck dinner at the house built by his great-great-great-grandfather. May 3, 2008.

INTRODUCTION

BILL KELLER

LONG BEFORE WE CHOSE THE ONE-WORD election night headline ("OBAMA"), long before we even knew who the nominees would be, we knew this would be unlike any election in a generation or two. The stakes — including the domestic vitality of the United States and its standing in the world — could not have been higher. The electorate was anxious, dispirited by years of feckless leadership, and polarized. The candidates ran the gamut ideologically and temperamentally and at various stages of the seemingly endless campaign at least half a dozen of those candidates were judged by the pollsters and pundits to have a real chance. Even the playing field had a way of changing: an election that, early on, seemed likely to hinge on the war in Iraq ended up revolving around fears of a feeble economy.

For news organizations, the spectacle presented additional challenges. One was the expense, not to mention the stamina, required to cover a campaign that began nearly two years before Election Day and involved a legion of candidates. The Times has always prided itself on sparing no necessary expense to cover the news, and we did not compromise on this one — except that reporters on this once-glamorous assignment lived a life of economy-class airplanes, Holiday Inns and Subway sandwiches. But with so many news organizations desperately slashing costs, Times reporters were sometimes the only ones who showed up in the early days, and there were fewer other reporters to share the pooled expenses of press buses and planes that, in the later stages of the campaign, follow the remaining candidates.

Another enlarged factor in our lives was the Internet, increasingly the resource of choice for political junkies — and as the season progressed, we were a nation of political junkies. In the presidential election four years earlier, nytimes.com had been a lively but decidedly junior partner to the printed paper. This time, we knew we would be judged at least as much for our performance on the Web as for our work in the paper. From the outset, we determined that our Web and print coverage would be one organic journalistic endeavor, produced by the same expert cast of reporters, editors, photographers, graphic artists, multimedia specialists and producers, exploiting the possibilities of both mediums. The result was a profusion of inventive features on the Web site — interactive electoral maps, first-class video, the immensely popular Caucus blog, online exchanges with readers — that complemented and enriched the deep reporting and analytical insight readers have always expected of The Times.

"All the News That's Fit to Print"

The New York Times

Late Edition

Today, limited sunshine, a shower, high 63. **Tonight,** cloudy, scattered showers, patchy fog, low 55. **Tomorrow,** rain ends, remaining cloudy, high 62. Weather map, Page B19.

VOL. CLVIII . . No. 54,485 + © 2008 The New York Times NEW YORK, WEDNESDAY, NOVEMBER 5, 2008 $5 beyond the greater New York metropolitan area. $1.50

OBAMA

RACIAL BARRIER FALLS IN DECISIVE VICTORY

DOUG MILLS/THE NEW YORK TIMES

President-elect Barack Obama with his wife, Michelle, and their daughters in Chicago on Tuesday night.

Democrats in Congress Strengthen Grip

By ADAM NAGOURNEY

Barack Hussein Obama was elected the 44th president of the United States on Tuesday, sweeping away the last racial barrier in American politics with ease as the country chose him as its first black chief executive.

The election of Mr. Obama amounted to a national catharsis — a repudiation of a historically unpopular Republican president and his economic and foreign policies, and an embrace of Mr. Obama's call for a change in the direction and the tone of the country.

But it was just as much a strikingly symbolic moment in the evolution of the nation's fraught racial history, a breakthrough that would have seemed unthinkable just two years ago.

Mr. Obama, 47, a first-term senator from Illinois, defeated Senator John McCain of Arizona, 72, a former prisoner of war who was making his second bid for the presidency.

To the very end, Mr. McCain's campaign was eclipsed by an opponent who was nothing short of a phenomenon, drawing huge crowds epitomized by the tens of thousands of people who turned out to hear Mr. Obama's victory speech in Grant Park in Chicago.

Mr. McCain also fought the headwinds of a relentlessly hostile political environment, weighted down with the baggage left to him by President Bush and an economic collapse that took place in the middle of the general election campaign.

"If there is anyone out there who still doubts that America is a place where all things are possible, who still wonders if the dream of our founders is alive in our time, who still questions the power of our democracy, tonight is your answer," said Mr. Obama, standing before a huge wooden lectern with a row of American flags at his back, casting his eyes to a crowd that stretched far into the Chicago night.

"It's been a long time coming," the president-elect added, "but tonight, because of what we did on this date in this election at this defining moment, change has come to America."

Mr. McCain delivered his concession speech under clear skies on the lush lawn of the Arizona Biltmore, in Phoenix, where he and his wife had held their wedding reception. The crowd reacted with scattered boos as he offered his congratulations to Mr. Obama and saluted the historical significance of the moment.

"This is a historic election, and I recognize the significance it has for African-Americans and for the special pride that must be theirs tonight," Mr. McCain said, adding, "We both realize that we have come a long way from the injustices that once stained our nation's reputation."

Not only did Mr. Obama capture the presidency, but he led his party to sharp gains in Congress. This puts

Continued on Page P3

08 ONLINE

- *The latest state-by-state results: the presidential contest and House, Senate and governors' races.*
- *The Caucus blog: updates from The Times's political staff.*

- *Interactive graphics: the electoral map, voter profiles and analysis.*
- *Video, audio and photos: reactions from the voters and the campaigns.*

nytimes.com

PRESIDENT-ELECT

THE LONG CAMPAIGN

Journey to the Top

The story of Senator Barack Obama's journey to the pinnacle of American politics is the story of a campaign that was, even in the view of many rivals, almost flawless. After a somewhat lackluster start, Mr. Obama and his team delivered. They developed a strategy to secure the nomination, and stuck with it even after setbacks. PAGE P1

SENATE

NORTH CAROLINA

Elizabeth Dole Is Out

After leading by a double-digit margin, the Republican Senator Elizabeth Dole, left, was defeated by State Senator Kay R. Hagan. In the campaign's final week, Mrs. Dole came under criticism for an advertisement that linked Ms. Hagan to a group called the Godless Americans. PAGE P12

VIRGINIA

Mark Warner Wins

Extending the Democrats' advantage in the Senate, former Gov. Mark R. Warner of Virginia easily won his race to replace John W. Warner (no relation), a retiring Republican. PAGE P12

NEW HAMPSHIRE

Sununu Is Defeated

Another leading Republican, Senator John E. Sununu, was ousted by a wide margin by Jeanne Shaheen, the former New Hampshire governor whom he beat in 2002. PAGE P12

HOUSE

CONNECTICUT

G.O.P. Stalwart Falls

Representative Christopher Shays, the last Republican House member from New England and a political Houdini who escaped previous Democratic attempts to topple him, was defeated by a political novice, Jim Himes. PAGE P15

NEW YORK

LEGISLATURE

Democrats Take Senate

Democrats won a majority in the New York State Senate, putting the party in control of both houses of the Legislature and the governor's office for the first time since the New Deal. Voters ousted two Republican senators whose combined years in office spanned more than half a century. PAGE P15

FOR HOME DELIVERY CALL 1-800-NYTIMES

THE CHALLENGE

No Time for Laurels; Now the Hard Part

By PETER BAKER

WASHINGTON — No president since before Barack Obama was born has ascended to the Oval Office confronted by the accumulation of seismic challenges awaiting him. Historians grasping for parallels point to Abraham Lincoln taking office as the nation was collapsing into Civil War, or Franklin D. Roosevelt arriving in Washington in the throes of the Great Depression.

The task facing Mr. Obama does not rise to those levels, but that these are the comparisons most often cited sobers even Democrats rejoicing at their return to power. On the shoulders of a 47-year-old first-term senator, with the power of inspiration yet no real executive experience, now falls the responsibility of prosecuting two wars, protecting the nation from terrorist threat and stitching back together a shredded economy.

Given the depth of these issues, Mr. Obama has little choice but to "put your arm around chaos," in the words of Leon E. Panetta, the former White House chief of staff who has been advising his transition team.

"You better damn well do the tough stuff up front, because if you think you can delay the tough decisions and tiptoe past the graveyard, you're in for a lot of trouble," Mr. Panetta said. "Make the decisions that involve pain and sacrifice up front."

What kind of decision maker and leader Mr. Obama will be remains unclear even to many of his supporters. Will he be willing to use his political capital and act boldly, or will he move cautiously and risk being paralyzed by competing demands from within his own party? His performance under the harsh lights of the campaign trail suggests a figure with remarkable coolness and confidence under enormous pressure, yet also one who rarely veers off the methodical path he lays out.

"It leads you to wonder whether passivity is the way he approaches most things," said John R. Bolton, President Bush's former ambassador to the United Na-

Continued on Page P4

THE MOMENT

After Decades, A Time to Reap

By KEVIN SACK

ALBANY, Ga. — Rutha Mae Harris backed her silver Town Car out of the driveway early Tuesday morning, pointed it toward her polling place on Mercer Avenue and started to sing.

"I'm going to vote like the spirit say vote," Miss Harris chanted softly.

I'm going to vote like the
spirit say vote,
I'm going to vote like the
spirit say vote,
And if the spirit say vote I'm
going to vote,
Oh Lord, I'm going to vote
when the spirit say vote.

As a 21-year-old student (on right in photo), she had bellowed that same freedom song at mass meetings at Mount Zion Baptist Church back in 1961, the year Barack Obama was born in Hawaii, a universe away. She sang it again while marching on Albany's City Hall, where she and other black students demanded the right to vote, and in the cramped and filthy cells of the city jail, which the Rev. Dr. Martin Luther King Jr. described as the worst he ever inhabited.

For those like Miss Harris who withstood jailings and beatings and threats to their livelihoods, all because they wanted to vote, the short drive to the polls on Tuesday culminated a lifelong journey from a time that is at once unrecognizable and eerily familiar here in southwest Georgia. As they exited the voting booths, some in wheelchairs, others with canes, these foot soldiers of the civil rights movement could not suppress either their jubilation or their astonishment at having voted for an African-American for president of the United States.

"They didn't give us our mule and our acre, but things are better," Miss Harris, 67, said with a gratified smile. "It's time to reap some of the harvest."

When Miss Harris arrived at the city gymnasium where she votes, her 80-year-old friend Mamie L. Nelson greeted her with a hug. "We marched, we sang and now it's happening," Ms. Nelson said. "It's really a feeling I

Continued on Page P6

THE PROMISE

For Many Abroad, An Ideal Renewed

By ETHAN BRONNER

GAZA — From far away, this is how it looks: There is a country out there where tens of millions of white Christians, voting freely, select as their leader a black man of modest origin, the son of a Muslim. There is a place on Earth — call it America — where such a thing happens.

Even where the United States is held in special contempt, like here in this benighted Palestinian coastal strip, the "glorious epic of Barack Obama," as the leftist French editor Jean Daniel calls it, makes America — the idea as much as the actual place — stand again, perhaps only fleetingly, for limitless possibility.

"It allows us all to dream a little," said Oswaldo Calvo, 58, a Venezuelan political activist in Caracas, in a comment echoed to correspondents of The New York Times on four continents in the days leading up to the election.

Tristram Hunt, a British historian, put it this way: Mr. Obama "brings the narrative that everyone wants to return to — that America is the land of extraordinary opportunity and possibility, where miracles happen."

But wonder is almost overwhelmed by relief. Mr. Obama's election offers most non-Americans a sense that the imperial power capable of doing such good and such harm — a country that, they complain, preached justice but tortured its captives, launched a disastrous war in Iraq, turned its back on the environment and greedily dragged the world into economic chaos — saw the errors of its ways over the past eight years and shifted course.

They say the country that weakened democratic forces abroad through a tireless but often ineffective campaign for democracy — dismissing results it found unsavory, cutting deals with dictators it needed as allies in its other battles — was now shining a transformative beacon with its own democratic exercise.

It would be hard to overstate how fervently vast

Continued on Page P4

The Obama campaign was known for its iconography, including these posters by Los Angeles street artist Shepard Fairey.

Our aim in a presidential election is much more than tracking a horse race. We try not just to recount the news, but to dig behind it, explain it. We try to represent the candidates in their own words, but also to truth-test their claims and counterclaims. We report their records and declared policies, but we pursue that more elusive quality, their characters. And we try to use the campaign as a window on America at a particular time. We do this by polling, of course, but also by sending reporters into the country to practice that precious and endangered art: listening. By listening in the black beauty parlors of the South, we caught the current of fear that accompanied the pride many African-Americans felt in the campaign of Barack Obama. By listening in the megachurches, we picked up the shift of evangelical Christians away from the angry dogma of old-line pulpit conservatives.

My belief that we did justice to the amazing story of Campaign 2008 is reinforced by the millions of viewers who flocked to our Web site at big moments in the campaign, and the thousands who lined up for copies of the newspaper the day after Election Day.

At times, our work stirred the ire of candidates and their followers. When we dug into her husband's business and philanthropic dealings, we drew howls from supporters of Senator Hillary Rodham Clinton's campaign. When we examined Senator John McCain's relationships with lobbyists and special interests, his campaign and its echo chamber charged that The Times was in league with Democrats. (They cranked up the volume even louder when we disclosed how superficially the McCain campaign vetted his running mate, Gov. Sarah Palin.) When we published a piece exploring Obama's tenuous connection to a 1960s radical, his supporters wailed that we were knuckling under to the Republicans.

This comes with the territory. Attacking the messenger is a time-honored way for a campaign distressed by a damaging story to change the subject. When the messenger is The Times, it is also a way of rousing that subset of the electorate for whom "New York" suggests "Sodom and Gomorrah," or whose knowledge of The Times rests entirely on a caricature presented by Rush Limbaugh and right-wing bloggers. And campaign strategists sometimes hope a loud denunciation will serve the same purpose as a pitcher brushing back an aggressive batter — make us a little more timid in our reporting. But the passions ran unusually high in this campaign, reflecting both the high stakes and the new media landscape we operate in.

When it comes to our job of afflicting the comfortable, we try to be equal opportunity afflicters. (You could ask such Democrats as Eliot Spitzer and Charlie Rangel, who endured some unwanted Times scrutiny in 2008.)

The Times employs editorial writers and columnists to voice their opinions, but they do not work in the newsroom and they answer to a different boss. Among news reporters and editors, fair play — the discipline to set aside any personal predilection and let readers be the judge — is regarded as a fundamental of the job. These days it sometimes feels as if we are defying gravity. The emotionally charged forum of the Web sometimes seems designed to reinforce the most fiercely held opinions; it is easy to swing from Web site to Web site, feeling informed without ever encountering information that challenges one's personal prejudices. And some old media seem to be following suit. Fox News, home of the most cynical slogan in the news business ("Fair and Balanced"), served as the house organ of the Republicans in Campaign 2008. MSNBC, sensing a rich market niche on the other side of the spectrum, created an evening lineup of cheerleaders for the Democrats.

At The Times, I think we did a pretty good job of keeping our balance. All of this coverage is preserved on our Web site. You can judge for yourselves.

Even rigorously impartial or downright jaded journalists were not immune to the excitement of this campaign's narrative, or the engrossing figure of its victorious protagonist. Whatever one thought of his politics, it was hard not to be captivated by the story of Barack Obama, an essentially American amalgam of Kenya and Kansas and Indonesia and Hawaii and Harvard and Chicago, a phenomenon we have not seen before in our politics but one that, after it was over, seemed almost inevitable.

We struggled and stretched for analogies in our political history. As a former foreign correspondent, I found myself thinking back to South Africa in 1994, when I covered the election of Nelson Mandela. It was not just the momentous racial breakthrough, nor just the surging passion of the crowds. It was the combination of discipline and inspiration, the pragmatic opportunism underlying the lofty sense of historic purpose. Whether Obama lives up to that analogy will be our job to discover in the years ahead.

This book is a distillation of two years' labor by a cast of journalists any editor would be honored to work with. Their dispatches have been refashioned into a single narrative by my sidekick, Jill Abramson, and joined to a showcase of splendid Times photojournalism. Those who deserve the real credit for this volume are named on page 238.

One brilliant veteran of many campaign trails was with us early on, but watched much of this campaign from a sickbed as her health flickered and dimmed. I think all of my colleagues would join me in dedicating this account to Robin Toner, with love.

IMAGES COURTESY OF SHEPARD FAIREY/OBEY GIANT

DAMON WINTER/NYT

WINDS OF CHANGE

"I think it's fair to say that the conventional wisdom was that we could not win. We didn't have enough money. We didn't have enough organization. There was no way that a skinny guy from the South Side with a funny name like Barack Obama could ever win . . ."

MARCH 18, 2004

Rutha Mae Harris (right) seconds after learning of the election of Barack Obama as the 44th president of the United States. November 4, 2008.

MOISES SAMAN FOR NYT

ABOUT THE TEXT

JILL ABRAMSON is the author of this narrative, but she has constructed it on behalf of The Times and in collaboration with colleagues who covered every step of the presidential campaign. Parts of her narrative are based on a series of biographical profiles The Times published under the collective title "The Long Run." In writing the text, Abramson drew freely from the analysis, reporting, ideas and verbatim phrases already published in The Times, as well as from her own impressions drawn from editing and reporting during the long campaign season. It would be hard to improve on the prose of Jodi Kantor, Janny Scott, Adam Nagourney or Kevin Sack, to cite but a few examples, so she has often not even tried. Because so much of the text comes by design from work that previously appeared in The Times, citations to specific articles are not included. Sources used from outside of The Times are attributed.

T HE LINES BEGAN FORMING WEEKS before the election: in Florida, where seniors feared there might be a repeat of the rampant confusion that marred the disputed 2000 voting; in Ohio, where unsubstantiated rumors swirled that polling places would shut their doors promptly at the appointed closing time, no matter if there were still lines of eligible voters waiting; in roadside casinos and laundromats dotting dusty Western highways.

The early voting lines were just one striking measure. In previous elections, some Americans had become blasé about their most precious right, but not this time.

Rutha Mae Harris backed her silver Town Car out of the driveway, pointed it toward her polling place on Mercer Avenue in Albany, Ga., and started to sing.

> *"I'm going to vote like the spirit say vote,"*
> *Miss Harris chanted softly.*
> *"I'm going to vote like the spirit say vote,*
> *I'm going to vote like the spirit say vote,*
> *And if the spirit say vote I'm going to vote,*
> *Oh Lord, I'm going to vote when the spirit say vote."*

As a young student, she had bellowed that same freedom song at mass meetings at Mount Zion Baptist Church back in 1961, the year Barack Obama was born in Hawaii, a universe away. She sang it again while marching on Albany's City Hall, where she and other black students demanded the right to vote, and in the cramped and filthy cells of the city jail, which the Rev. Dr. Martin Luther King Jr. described as the worst he ever inhabited.

For many black Americans like Miss Harris, now 67, the short drive to the polls on November 4 culminated a lifelong journey. As they exited the voting booths, some in wheelchairs, others with canes, these foot soldiers of the civil rights movement could not suppress either their jubilation or their astonishment at having voted for an African-American for president of the United States.

Election workers in front of a voting station in La Madera, N.M. November 4, 2008.

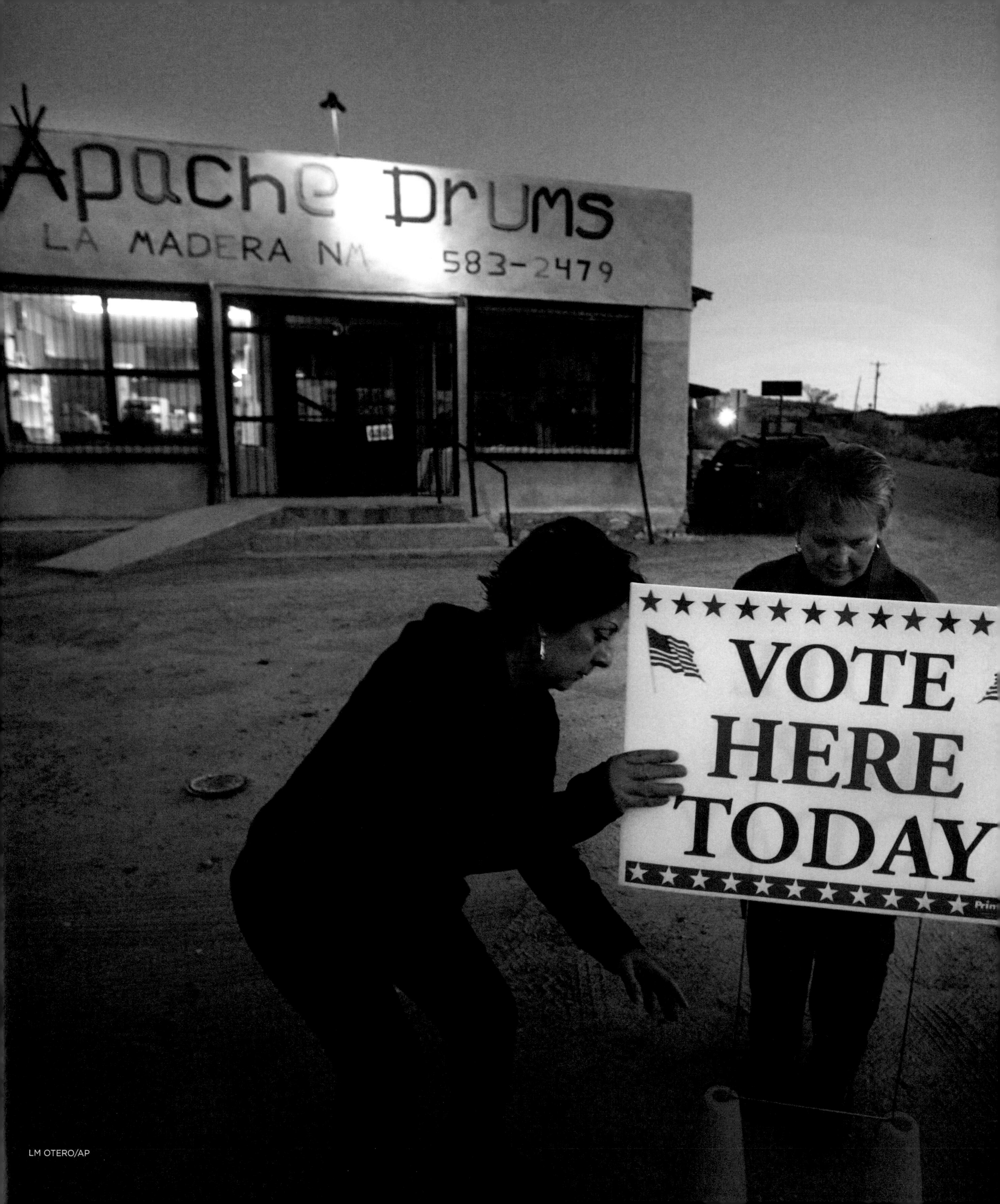

LM OTERO/AP

Obama supporters on Election Day, Athens, Ohio. November 4, 2008.

Hours earlier, just before 6 a.m., Kimberly Ferguson was 12th in line outside the Adam Clayton Powell State Office Building on 125th Street in Harlem. She was steps from the legendary Apollo Theater, where, in the fall of 2007, Barack Obama had spoken to an audience notably light on New York's black political leadership, who were backing Hillary Clinton.

"I got here early so I could make it to class," Ferguson said, shouldering a backpack of books with an orange peeking out of its side pocket. The Lehman College sophomore was part of a new army of young voters drawn to political participation through the Internet. All of her friends were voting, mostly for the first time, for Obama. "I want to be part of history," she said, as she clutched her voter registration form and watched carefully as an elderly woman in a leopard jacket and black cat-eye glasses tinkered with the voting machine.

> *"I want to be part of history," she said, as she clutched her voter registration form.*

Everywhere, there was a sense of history being made, not simply because of Barack Obama's meteoric rise, his unusual background and the campaign he ran but equally because the country was facing such daunting problems; a financial crisis like none seen since the Depression and two wars. Because so much was riding on the outcome, it felt like the world was holding its breath waiting for the vote.

At 7:36 a.m. banks of television cameras captured Barack and Michelle Obama as they arrived to vote, with their daughters, Malia, 10, and Sasha, 7, at Chicago's Beulah Shoesmith Elementary School. A few nights earlier, on Halloween, the candidate had briefly lost his cool when the cameras came too close while he walked Sasha, dressed as a corpse bride, to a neighborhood party. From this point onward, the Obamas and their young girls would be the focus of the kind of celebrity glare not seen since the Kennedys.

Celebration at the Obama family homestead in western Kenya after the election results are announced. November 5, 2008.

The candidate jokes with his daughters, Malia, left, and Sasha, in Fort Wayne, Ind. May 4, 2008.

DOUG MILLS/NYT

This was one reason Michelle Obama had taken so long to get comfortable with the idea of her husband running for president. "Barack and Michelle thought long and hard about this decision before they made it," said their good friend Valerie Jarrett. Michelle wanted her girls to have the kind of close family life that she and her brother Craig had enjoyed growing up on Chicago's South Side. There had been all too few family dinners since February 10, 2007, when, standing in the shadow of Abraham Lincoln's Old State Capitol in Springfield, Ill., Barack Obama had declared his candidacy for president and recognized "there is a certain presumptuousness — a certain audacity — to this announcement."

Then a follow-up question so sensible it could only come from a first-grader, "Shouldn't you be vice president first?"

Even Malia had found her father's fast rise audacious. Visiting the U.S. Capitol shortly after his election to the Senate in 2004, she asked whether he would try to be president. Then a follow-up question so sensible it could only come from a first-grader, "Shouldn't you be vice president first?" The Clintons and other Democratic elders grumbled that his experience was too slight to go up against a grizzled Republican veteran like John McCain. Vernon Jordan and other senior leaders of the civil rights movement implored him to wait his turn. Obama responded by quoting Martin Luther King Jr. on "the fierce urgency of now."

Eventually audacity became more than hope, with poll after poll showing a commanding Obama lead. In the closing days of the election, the campaign plane touched down in red states that hadn't gone Democratic since the Lyndon Johnson landslide of 1964 — even Confederate states like Virginia. Still, some commentators were continuing to warn about a so-called Bradley effect, where in the privacy of the voting booth whites who told the pollsters otherwise would never pull the lever for a black candidate. Top campaign aides worried that the Obama base was becoming overconfident. There were no sure bets in American politics.

"In his speech here on Saturday, Mr. Obama, trying to offer himself as the grass-roots outsider in contrast to a member of a political family that has dominated Washington life for 15 years, presented his campaign as an effort 'not just to hold an office, but to gather with you to transform a nation.'"

—From "Obama Formally Enters Presidential Race" by Adam Nagourney and Jeff Zeleny, The New York Times, February 11, 2007

Obama with his daughter Malia in front of a statue of James Madison at the Library of Congress. January 4, 2005.

On election night, Barack and Michelle shared a steak dinner at home, then joined their Chicago inner circle at a downtown hotel suite. There were the two Davids, Axelrod and Plouffe, the architects of the campaign's field strategies and advertising respectively, as well as the communications director Robert Gibbs. Jarrett, who had served as a mentor to both Barack and Michelle and, like them, was part of Chicago's black professional elite, embraced her friends. Children — the Obama girls and the grandchildren of Obama's running mate, Joseph R. Biden Jr.— bounced around the room.

According to Newsweek, Obama said, "It looks like we're going to win this thing, huh?"

Some of the key battleground states had already been called, but as the urban areas of Ohio began coming in, the candidate turned to Axelrod, a former political writer for the Chicago Sun-Times, who had been with him since he had been in the Illinois Senate.

According to Newsweek, Obama said, "It looks like we're going to win this thing, huh?"

"Yeah," nodded the red-eyed consultant.

In anticipation of a historic acceptance speech, crowds had been gathering in Chicago's Grant Park since daybreak.

Thousands of miles away, in the Kenyan village where Obama's father was born and buried, men and women sat entranced. "We're going to the White House," sang the large crowd gathered there, swatting mosquitoes as they watched the election results trickle in on fuzzy-screened television sets.

The rest of the world watched, too. In Gaza, where the United States is held in special contempt, it seemed scarcely possible that there could be a country where tens of millions of white Christians, voting freely, might select as their leader a black man of modest origin, the son of a Muslim. There is a place on Earth — call it America — where such a thing could happen.

And in Albany, Ga., Rutha Mae Harris was waiting and watching at Obama headquarters. ♦

America's new First Family at the Election Day rally in Grant Park, Chicago. November 4, 2008.

CHAPTER ONE

BEGINNINGS

"I learned to slip back and forth between my black and white worlds . . . convinced that with a bit of translation on my part the two worlds would eventually cohere."

"DREAMS FROM MY FATHER"

Barack Obama's parents, Barack Sr. and Stanley Ann Dunham, in Hawaii, 1971.

I N HIS MEMOIR, "DREAMS FROM MY Father," Barack Obama conjures up an imagined meeting between his white Kansas-born mother and his black Kenyan father that could have come straight out of the iconic, if hopelessly dated, 1960s movie "Guess Who's Coming to Dinner."

In 1960 such a meeting took place in Hawaii, where his mother's parents, Stanley and Madelyn Dunham, prepared to meet their daughter's beau, an African student reaching toward Phi Beta Kappa, whom she had met in Russian class.

The parents, Barack Obama's beloved "Gramps" and "Toot," were wary. Although Hawaii was a place of rich ethnic blends, racial tensions were still simmering, like those evident in "Guess Who's Coming to Dinner," where white liberals like the couple portrayed by Spencer Tracy and Katharine Hepburn nonetheless cringed over the prospect of a black son-in-law.

The Dunhams' new son-in-law-to-be, Barack (meaning "blessed"), was from the small village of Nyang'oma Kogelo near Lake Victoria. Now an economics student with a polished British accent, as a boy Barack helped tend his family's goats and attended school in a small shack. If the Dunhams were unsettled by the match between Barack Sr. and their daughter, 18-year-old Stanley Ann (her father had wanted a boy and she was named for him), Obama's family in Africa was apoplectic over the prospect of its blood being "sullied by a white woman," as Barack notes in "Dreams From My Father."

In 1961, the short-lived marriage produced a son, also named Barack. But the father soon abandoned his young family to attend Harvard, and then returned to Africa. The son would see his father only once again, when he was 10. Barack Sr. had a new life, wives and children back in Kenya as well as new demons, including depression and alcohol. One crippling car accident was followed by another, this time fatal, his short life ending in Nairobi at age 46 in 1982. As her son became a young adult, Ann tried to explain his father's life to him. In "Dreams From My Father" he writes that "she saw my father as everyone hopes at least one other person might see him; she tried to help the child who never knew him see him the same way. And it was the look on her face that day that I would remember when a few months later I called to tell her that my father had died and heard her cry out over the distance."

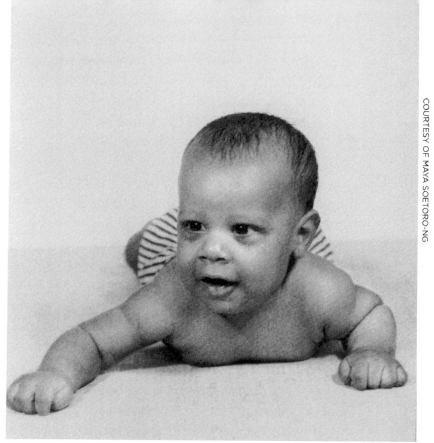

Baby Barack.

Playing in the ocean in the 1960s.

Out for a spin on his tricycle in the 1960s in Hawaii.

AN ABSENT FATHER

Father and son in the 1970s.

Ten-year old Barack Obama was filled with dread in 1971 when he was reunited with his father for the one and only time, in Honolulu during the Christmas season. Without consultation, a visit had been arranged for the African economist to speak to Barack's class at the elite prep school Punahou. "I couldn't imagine worse news," he wrote in his memoir. "I spent that night and all of the next day trying to suppress thoughts of the inevitable: the faces of my classmates when they heard about mud huts, all my lies exposed, the painful jokes afterward."

Barack was still the new kid at Punahou. The classroom visit, as it turned out, went well enough (one student told Barack he thought his father was "cool") but the monthlong family reunion was sometimes strained. His father, who needed a cane to walk, was frailer than his son anticipated, with the yellow eyes of someone who had endured malaria. He was also strict. When he thought Barack was ignoring his studies and watching too much television, a family fight that involved his mother and grandparents erupted over whether Barack would be allowed to watch the rest of "How the Grinch Stole Christmas." Barack did not believe his father had earned the right to become the house disciplinarian.

There were pleasant times, too, including a visit to a jazz club

> *There were pleasant times, too, including a visit to a jazz club and the Christmas gift of an orange basketball.*

and the Christmas gift of an orange basketball, bits and pieces of the brief relationship. "When I reach back into my memory for the words of my father," Obama wrote in "Dreams From My Father," "the small interactions or conversations we have had, they seem irretrievably lost."

In Africa, Barack Sr. had married another white woman and had two more children, as well as other children with Kenyan wives. But his unhappiness and drinking grew. Although he had worked successfully for an oil company and the government, he ended up on a government blacklist. A car accident in Kenya, in which he had been drinking and driving, had killed another man and left Obama Sr. in the hospital for nearly a year.

During his visit with Ann and Barack, he broached the idea of getting the family, including Ann's daughter with another man, Maya, back together. But even though Ann had broken up with her second husband, she rebuffed Barack's father.

Before his departure, the father had one last lesson for the boy. "Come, Barry, you will learn from the master," he said, as he retrieved two dusty 45 r.p.m. records from his suitcase and put them on the stereo. "Suddenly his slender body was swaying back and forth, the lush sound was rising." And the son began to dance.

Mother and son in the 1960s.

After divorcing Barack Sr., Ann had remarried, to another foreign student, Lolo Soetoro, of Indonesia, who was attending the University of Hawaii. After Soetoro's student visa was revoked, the family moved to Jakarta, where Barack was joined by a half-sister, Maya, with whom he remains close. He attended an Indonesian school, although campaign attacks suggesting it was militantly Islamic were patently false. To make sure her son kept up his English, Ann would wake him hours before school began to study a correspondence course. When Barack balked at her 4 a.m. home-schooling program, he recalled, her response was, "This is no picnic for me either, Buster."

His grandfather saw the school as his grandson's meal ticket.

Soetoro bought Barack boxing gloves and taught him how to fend off bullies. Ann, a flower child who viewed every black man, including her son, as the next Thurgood Marshall, began bringing home books and records by great black Americans.

But this blended family, too, soon cracked and Ann returned to Hawaii to be near her parents. Through his boss, Barack's "Gramps" had arranged for him to enter fifth grade at Punahou, a prep school founded by missionaries. His grandfather saw the school as his grandson's meal ticket and Barack said he told him "that the contacts I made at Punahou would last a lifetime, that I would move in charmed circles and have all the opportunities that he'd never had."

Barack's sojourn at the school, where there were few other blacks, included learning the folkways of the American elite, grounding that would be helpful at other academic proving grounds, like Columbia University and Harvard Law School. He excelled on the basketball court, with a jump shot that earned him the nickname "Barry O'Bomber" (Barack went by "Barry" for much of childhood). When his mother returned to Indonesia to do field work for her doctoral degree, Obama remained with his grandparents to finish his studies at Punahou.

"The political narrative of Mr. Obama was written about 4,500 miles and a cultural universe away from here, largely in Illinois. But the seeds of his racial consciousness, its attendant alienation and political curiosity appear to have been planted in Hawaii."

—*From "Charisma and a Search for Self in Obama's Hawaii Childhood" by Jennifer Steinhauer, The New York Times, March 17, 2007*

Stanley Dunham, Stanley Ann, Maya and Barack in the early 1970s.

THE WOMAN WHO SHAPED HIM

The high school student in 1960.

The mother in the 1970s.

The anthropologist in 1988.

Despite his father's large presence in "Dreams From My Father," Barack Obama's unconventional, free-spirited mother, Stanley Ann Dunham Soetoro, was the parent who most shaped him.

When he speaks of her, his words seem tinged with a mix of love and regret. Oceans and continents sometimes divided them. His half-sister, Maya Soetoro-Ng, has said that Soetoro's most difficult decision was to leave her son to finish high school in Hawaii while she pursued her studies in Indonesia. "She wanted him to be with her," Soetoro-Ng recalled. But she also recognized that while it was painful to be separated, "it was perhaps the best thing for him."

Obama has said his biggest mistake was not being at his mother's bedside when she died. And when The Associated Press asked the candidates about "prized keepsakes" — others mentioned signed baseballs or a pocket watch — Obama said his was a photograph of the cliffs of the South Shore of Oahu in Hawaii where his mother's ashes were scattered. "I know that she was the kindest, most generous spirit I have ever known, and that what is best in me I owe to her," he wrote.

"I think sometimes that had I known she would not survive her illness, I might have written a different book — less a meditation on the absent parent, more a celebration of the one who was the single constant in my life," he wrote in the preface to "Dreams From My Father." She spent her last months of life in 1995 struggling with ovarian cancer, worrying about how to pay her health bills and reading his manuscript.

Maya Soetoro-Ng has described a woman who had high

> *"I know that she was the kindest, most generous spirit I have ever known, and that what is best in me I owe to her."*

expectations for her children, hated bigotry and loved "life's gorgeous minutiae," such as the peasant blacksmithing in Java about which she wrote an 800-page dissertation. Her philosophy of life, according to her daughter, was to "not build walls around ourselves."

"She was a very, very big thinker," said Nancy Barry, a former president of Women's World Banking, an international network of microfinance providers, where Soetoro worked in New York City in the early 1990s. "She was not afraid to speak truth to power."

She became a consultant for the United States Agency for International Development on setting up a village credit program, then a Ford Foundation program officer in Jakarta specializing in women's work. Later, she was a consultant in Pakistan, then joined Indonesia's oldest bank to work on what is described as the world's largest sustainable microfinance program, creating services like credit and savings for the poor.

When Obama was in high school, she confronted him about his seeming lack of ambition, Obama wrote. He could get into any college in the country, she told him, with just a little effort. ("Remember what that's like? Effort?") He says he looked at her, so earnest and sure of his destiny: "I suddenly felt like puncturing that certainty of hers, letting her know that her experiment with me had failed."

Of course, the experiment was hardly a failure. "There were certainly times in his life in those four years when he could have used her presence on a more daily basis," said Soetoro-Ng, who became an anthropologist like her mother. "But I think he did all right for himself."

Barack Obama throws a lei at the spot where he once scattered his mother's ashes, Honolulu. August 14, 2008.

In "Dreams From My Father," Obama writes candidly about the struggle for identity that defined his boyhood. At school he heard a coach use the word "nigger," and his own beloved grandmother, "Toot" (his rendering of an abbreviation for "Tutu," which means "grandparent" in Hawaiian), would occasionally utter "racial or ethnic stereotypes that made me cringe," Obama recalled in his campaign speech on race. He had a pack of close friends and exhibited behavior, including drinking and smoking marijuana, typical of male teenagers. His mother and grandparents worried that he was lackadaisical about his studies, but Barack had begun a habit of disappearing behind his bedroom door to read for hours, shuttered with Richard Wright, James Baldwin and Malcolm X, and "there I would sit," he wrote in his memoir, "and wrestle with words, locked suddenly in desperate argument, trying to reconcile the world as I'd found it with the terms of my birth."

"Barry O'Bomber" at Punahou School in Hawaii, 1979.

COURTESY OF OBAMA FOR AMERICA

In "Dreams From My Father," Obama writes candidly about the struggle for identity that defined his boyhood.

His quest for identity continued at the small California liberal arts Occidental College, known for its diverse student body, and also at Columbia, where he transferred after two years. Obama spent his first night in New York City curled up in an alleyway, waiting to move into his apartment in Spanish Harlem. The precariousness of his place in the world, the sense that his life could have easily slipped into the stereotype of black male failure, pervades "Dreams From My Father":

"Junkie. Pothead. That's where I'd been headed: the final, fatal role of the young would-be black man."

When The Times investigated Obama's use of drugs during this period of his life, the paper found that it seemed to be less of an issue than Obama portrayed in his book, where he said he used drugs to help numb the confusion he felt about himself and described partying, smoking "reefer" and doing a little "blow." But Amiekoleh Usafi, a friend from Occidental, said the most she saw Obama indulging in were cigarettes and beer. Others interviewed had similar accounts.

During his Occidental and Columbia years, Obama grew more politically aware, becoming involved in student anti-apartheid groups. After Columbia, he had difficulty getting hired as a community organizer, the job he wanted, and worked for a year at a business where he wore a suit and could have started down a path toward money and status.

On the streets of Chicago's South Side, Obama came to terms with his place in black America.

But in 1985, Gerald Kellman, a community organizer in Chicago's tough South Side, interviewed a young applicant who "challenged me on whether we would teach him anything," Kellman recalled. "He wanted to know things like 'How are you going to train me?' and 'What am I going to learn?'" With a $10,000 salary and $2,000 Kellman gave him to buy a used car, Obama began a three-year stint as a grassroots organizer in Chicago's projects and churches.

It is a period that looms large in "Dreams From My Father," where Obama recounts the frustrations and triumphs of getting asbestos removed from the apartments at Altgeld Gardens and learning the political skills needed to mediate anger and deal with urban poverty. He vividly recounts his disappointment with himself when he is unable to control a group of residents whose anger boils over at a tense meeting with city officials. But the job, he wrote, was "the best education I ever had, better than anything I got at Harvard Law School." On the streets of Chicago's South Side, Obama came to terms with his place in black America. "All of a sudden Barack finds himself in one of the most complex African-American communities in the United States and he discovers an energizing capacity to connect with the people in these neighborhoods," said Gregory Galluzo, a community organizer who worked with Obama.

Obama practiced some of the methods of Saul Alinsky, a Chicago native regarded as the father of community organizing, who argued for working through cultural institutions like churches and synagogues. In the '60s, a Wellesley senior had written an eloquent thesis about Alinsky's teachings. Her name was Hillary Rodham, the future Hillary Rodham Clinton. ♦

Obama spent his last two years of college in New York City, where he attended Columbia University. Here he is shown in Central Park, 1983.

A GRANDMOTHER'S LOVE

*Obama with his grandmother, Madelyn Dunham,
after he graduated high school, 1979.*

For the last 21 months, she had followed the odyssey of his presidential campaign like a spectator on a faraway balcony.

She underwent a corneal transplant to better see him on television. In one of their frequent telephone conversations she told him that it might not hurt if he smiled a bit more.

And, just 11 days before the election, Barack Obama suspended his campaign to spend a day in Honolulu saying goodbye.

At the Punahou Circle Apartments, Madelyn Dunham, his grandmother, lay gravely ill. For weeks, Obama had talked to doctors and tracked her condition. She suffered from cancer and other ailments. When she was released from the hospital after surgery to repair a broken hip, he received word that he should not wait until after the election to make a likely final visit.

He told his campaign advisers that the trip was not negotiable. He was not there when his mother died in 1995, a mistake he said he did not intend to repeat with her mother, a stalwart in his life. She lay in the same apartment where Obama lived from the age of 10, now flooded with flowers and good wishes from strangers who wrote that they had come to know her from "Dreams From My Father." His sister, Maya, was also there.

"One of the things I wanted to make sure of is that I had a chance to sit down with her and talk to her," Obama said on the ABC News television program "Good Morning America." "She's still alert and she's still got all her faculties, and I want to make sure that — that I don't miss that opportunity right now."

"She is getting a sense of long-deserved recognition at — towards the end of her life," he added.

As Obama flew west across six time zones on his way to see her, he remained secluded in the front cabin of his campaign plane. It was a starkly different mood from that during a flight nine months earlier, when Obama made a pilgrimage to Kansas for his first visit to the town of El Dorado, where his maternal grandparents had originally lived. The campaign liked to flaunt his Kansas roots and his grandfather's military service during World War II to show off the apple-pie American part of his background.

A smile washed over his face on that late January day as he spoke about the woman he called Toot.

"She can't travel," he told reporters then. "She has a bad back. She has pretty severe osteoporosis. But she's glued to CNN."

In the opening stages of his Democratic primary fight, Obama spoke wistfully about his grandparents, whose all-American biography had become critical to establishing his own American story. He told of how his grandfather, Stanley, who died in 1992, had fought in World War II while his grandmother worked on B-29s at a Boeing plant in Wichita.

"My grandparents held on to a simple dream: that they would raise my mother in a land of boundless dreams," Obama said. "I am standing here today because that dream was realized."

In only one campaign commercial, made during the primary race, can Dunham be heard speaking. Her osteoporosis was advanced, and she hunched so severely that it was hard for the filmmakers to capture her spirit and words of support for her grandson.

In August, as he prepared to accept the Democratic nomination, Obama delivered a long-distance message to her in a televised speech.

"Thank you to my grandmother, who helped raise me and is sitting in Hawaii somewhere right now because she can't travel, but who poured everything she had into me and who helped me become the man I am today," Obama said. "Tonight is for her."

Sadly, Dunham, 86, who watched from afar as her only grandson rapidly ascended the ranks of American politics to the brink of the presidency, did not live to see him elected.

"She has gone home," Obama announced at a late campaign stop in North Carolina the day before the election. His voice was tinged with emotion. "She died peacefully in her sleep with my sister at her side, so there's great joy instead of tears."

> *Barack Obama suspended his campaign to spend a day in Honolulu saying goodbye.*

The candidate weeps while speaking of his grandmother during a rally in Charlotte, N.C. She had died earlier, just a day short of his election. November 3, 2008.

From Barry to Barack, and Beyond

ROGER COHEN

To his former classmates at the Besuki elementary school in Jakarta, Indonesia, Barack Obama was the kid in Bermudas who joined their fourth-grade class in 1970. The boy was then called Barry Soetoro (the family name of Obama's Indonesian stepfather). No wonder it took his Indonesian friends a long time to recognize that the chubby kid who ate sandwiches rather than noodles and the skinny guy now elected as America's 44th president were one and the same.

Many people around the world have been rubbing their eyes at Obama. His emergence seems providential; he's the post-racial barrier-breaker for the Age of Connectedness. As his name change suggests, Obama has spent his life building bridges to assemble a coherent identity. A post-9/11 world in which everything is global except politics needs some of that conciliatory reflex.

With a Kenyan father, an American mother and a Muslim grandfather, the new president speaks to a world in flux, where growing numbers of people live between places rather than in a single spot. From Malaysia to Mexico, Obama seems somehow familiar. He looks more like the guy at the local bodega than the guys on dollar bills.

But there is more to global "Obamania." His accessibility follows a season of U.S. remoteness. America has been the bellicose power speaking not of possibility but of punishment, hunched where it was open-armed. The U.S. betrayal of its own ideals, for which Abu Ghraib and Guantánamo are now synonyms, has caused immense bitterness.

> From Malaysia to Mexico, Obama seems somehow familiar. He looks more like the guy at the local bodega than the guys on dollar bills.

It's legitimate to ask why. The answer can only be that so much hope is still vested in the American ideal. China and India may be rising but their ascendancy has not brought any magnetic new message. Hope in America is not illogical. It is based on a U.S. story of renewal and generous sacrifice. The United States is a transformational power or it is nothing. As Richard Hofstadter has observed, "It has been our fate as a nation not to have ideologies, but to be one." Obama, by becoming the first African-American president, has restored the mythology of American possibility.

But he will govern in the real world: one of recession, rising unemployment, two intractable wars in Afghanistan and Iraq, energy challenges and unforeseeable threats. There will be disappointments and misjudgments. Still, on the basis of everything we know about him, Obama will learn from them. If he can hone his instinct for dialogue, he may succeed in dislodging a few relationships from their current frozen antagonism: with Iran, with Syria, with Cuba. The map of the world would then change. He will have to be the jujitsu president, turning apparent American weaknesses into new forms of strength.

It was on my last visit to Indonesia, the world's most populous Muslim nation, that I met Obama's former classmates with their enthusiasm for the president-elect. The time before, in 2005, I spoke to Sholeh Ibrahim, a teacher in an Islamic religious boarding school. His rage against America overflowed. "I am angry with President Bush who sees Islam as an enemy," he told me. "When we are attacked, we must fight back."

These two images, separated by three years, reflect the love and hatred that the United States is capable of inspir-

YAN PEI-MING

ing in unique degree. No other nation so inhabits the global imagination. But the images also reflect something else: two kinds of Islam, a moderate form typical of the soft contours of tropical Indonesia, and a more fanatical fringe. Distinguishing such differences is not just about words, it is a matter of experience. Nuance comes alive when lived. The world never believed Bush experienced a nuance he could identify, with respect to Islam or anything else.

But Obama, forced through his upbringing to explore the spaces in between — the areas that are neither black nor white, neither "with us" nor "against us" — has grown, and come to power, by uniting disparate threads. Only thus could he move, whole, from Barry Soetoro to Barack Obama. An interconnected globe now awaits a further Obama osmosis, ushering in the promise of the 21st century beyond the war on terror. ◆

Barack Obama as a student at Harvard Law School.

CHAPTER TWO

THE MAKING OF A POLITICIAN

"Whether people were friendly, indifferent or occasionally hostile, I tried my best to keep my mouth shut and hear what they had to say."

"THE AUDACITY OF HOPE"

DOERS' PROFILE:

Barrage O'Trauma

Age:	Extraordinarily mature
Occupation:	First African African-American President of a major law revue published outside of New Haven.
Latest Accomplishments:	Faking Macho Sports Injury To Ensure Election Limiting Body Meetings to 2 ½ Hours Deflecting Persistent Questioning About Ring On Left Hand
Last Books Read:	Everything I Know I Learned in Kindergarten Modern Folk Tales
Why I Do What I Do:	"To contribute to legal scholarship, sharpen my mind, . . . and the ladies love it."
Quote:	"Engage, empower, smoke Marlboro."
Profile:	Shy, awkward, insecure. Not interested in politics.
His Scotch:	Doers White Label. "Six or seven bottles makes even McConnell go down smooth.

An issue of the Harvard Law Review contained a parody of Barack Obama.

"Dreams from My Father" ends with Barack Obama's first journey to Kenya, where he went after receiving his acceptance letter from Harvard Law School. He met his half-brothers and half-sisters, forging new relationships with his father's African family, including his step-grandmother, Sarah, who helped raise his father in the same way his grandmother, Toot, looked after Barack.

He was older than the other first-year students at Harvard and at the end of the year he won a coveted slot as one of about 80 editors of the prestigious law review, the most influential in the country. That summer, he worked as an associate at the Chicago firm of Sidley & Austin where he met and fell in love with another young Harvard Law grad, Michelle Robinson. They continued a long-distance courtship.

The next year, in February 1990, after a deliberation that took 17 hours, he won the law review's presidency with support from politically conservative students. Weeks before the voting he had made a speech in favor of affirmative action that so eloquently summarized the arguments against it that conservatives believed he would give their concerns a fair shake.

Obama sometimes joked that the presidency of the Harvard Law Review was the second-hardest elective office in the country to win. He was the first black elected in its 104-year history and the election made him an instant celebrity, including a profile in The New York Times.

"The fact that I've been elected shows a lot of progress," he told Times correspondent Fox Butterfield. "But it's important that stories like mine aren't used to say that everything is O.K. for blacks. You have to remember that for every one of me, there are hundreds or thousands of black students with at least equal talent who don't get a chance," he said, alluding to poverty or growing up in a drug environment.

The Harvard Law Review Board of Editors for the 1990-1991 academic year. Obama is at center, holding the staff.

After law school, Obama returned to Chicago, where he ran a voter registration drive in 1992.

From Harvard he returned to Chicago, where he worked on a voter registration drive, started work at a small law firm specializing in civil rights cases and taught at the University of Chicago Law School. In 1992, he and Michelle were married.

A Harvard Law connection, Michael W. McConnell, a conservative scholar who is now a federal appellate judge who had been impressed by Obama's editing of an article he wrote at Harvard, put him on the path to a fellowship at the law school, which provided an office and a computer, which he used to write "Dreams From My Father."

He joined Trinity United Church of Christ, led by the Rev. Jeremiah A. Wright Jr.

Obama taught three courses, the most original of which was a historical and political seminar on racism and the law. He refined his public speaking style. He was wary of noble theories, his students said. He was, rather, a contextualist, willing to look past legal niceties to get results.

Religion had begun playing a role in his life before he went to Harvard, and he had joined Trinity United Church of Christ, led by the Rev. Jeremiah A. Wright Jr., who later presided at his marriage to Michelle. One of the pastor's sermons had inspired both the title of Obama's second book and his keynote speech at the 2004 Democratic convention, "The Audacity of Hope."

Politics was very much on his mind as Barack Obama cemented his ties to Hyde Park, the Chicago neighborhood with a long history of electing reform-minded politicians. A tight-knit community that runs through the South Side, Hyde Park is a liberal bastion of integration in what is otherwise one of the nation's most segregated cities. At its heart is the University of Chicago, where Obama also began cultivating connections to the city's white legal elite, including Democrats like former U.S. Judge Abner J. Mikva and the former chairman of the Federal Communications Commission, Newton Minow. "He felt completely comfortable in Hyde Park," said Martha Minow, Newton's daughter and Obama's former law professor and mentor.

"**M**ost aspiring politicians do not dwell in the halls of academia, and few promising young legal thinkers toil in state legislatures. Mr. Obama planted a foot in each, splitting his weeks between an elite law school and the far less rarefied atmosphere of the Illinois Senate."

—From "Teaching Law, Testing Ideas, Obama Stood Slightly Apart" by Jodi Kantor, The New York Times, July 30, 2008

Illinois State Senator Barack Obama at a community meeting in his district.

Teaching at the University of Chicago.

In 1992, Obama led a successful registration drive that added nearly 150,000 black voters and helped elect Carol Moseley Braun, a Democrat and the first African-American woman in the U.S. Senate. In 1995, Obama kicked off his candidacy for the Illinois Senate at the same Hyde Park hotel where Harold Washington, the city's first black mayor, had announced his candidacy.

> *Like other members of a new class of black political leaders, he tended to speak about race indirectly or implicitly, when he spoke about it at all.*

He did not fit the profile of the typical black politician. He had not grown up in the traditions of the American black church and he was younger than the generation of civil rights leaders for whom Birmingham and Selma were defining moments. He had thrived in white institutions with a style more conciliatory than confrontational, more technocrat than preacher. Like other members of a new class of black political leaders, he tended to speak about race indirectly or implicitly, when he spoke about it at all.

In a state where the Democratic machine still dominated local politics, he was an independent progressive. But once in the Senate, he learned to straddle all of these worlds. He found a mentor in an old-style boss, State Senator Emil Jones Jr., a black leader of the older generation.

In a South Shore neighborhood during Obama's 1995 run for Illinois State Senate.

PHOTOS: MARK LYONS FOR NYT

SOUTH SIDE GIRL

She was "The Rock" and "The Closer." Michelle Obama, of Princeton and Harvard Law, was equally the tough girl navigating the streets of South Side Chicago. Before her husband gave the keynote speech that brought down the House at the Democratic convention in 2004 she told him, "Just don't screw it up, buddy." Before she would give her blessing for the presidential run, she extracted one last condition: he would have to give up smoking.

More than many other candidates, Barack Obama openly talked about the strains the campaign put on his family. At one of the final debates, his voice cracked when he talked about leaving his girls to fly back to Washington for a vote. In 2006, at a Washington book party to celebrate the publication of "The Audacity of Hope," he became tearful while recognizing the sacrifices his family had made for his career. When he couldn't continue, Michelle came up, threw her arms around him and kissed his tearful cheeks.

The newlyweds spend Christmas in Hawaii, 1992.

Michelle in grade school.

Like her husband, the 45-year-old lawyer and hospital administrator can be a dazzling speaker. Andrew Rosenthal, the editorial page editor of The New York Times, saw her perform at a rally in Los Angeles with Caroline Kennedy, Maria Shriver and Oprah Winfrey. The Times had endorsed Hillary Clinton in the primaries, but it was Michelle who wowed Rosenthal. "Forty-eight hours before the closest thing America has ever had to a national primary, four extraordinary women put on the best campaign rally I've seen in 20 years of covering presidential politics," he wrote.

Her bluntness and humor drew praise, though Times columnist Maureen Dowd also saw, earlier than almost anyone, the potential for pitfalls. Dowd wasn't so crazy about Michelle's public chidings of her husband for not putting the butter back in the fridge or for not putting his dirty socks in the laundry.

And soon, controversy did flare. In Madison, Wis., in February, Michelle told voters that hope was sweeping America, adding, "For the first time in my adult lifetime, I am really proud of my country." The words replayed in an endless loop of cable outrage and she was quickly caricatured as The Angry Black Woman.

Although she said she could have better expressed herself, Michelle was upset at the way her words were twisted. "You are amazed sometimes at how deep the lies can be," she said.

Wedding day, October 18, 1992.

Michelle Obama talks to potential voters at a call center in Akron, Ohio. October 24, 2008.

Michelle Obama on stage with daughters Malia, left, and Sasha during the Democratic National Convention in Denver. August 25, 2008.

ROBYN BECK/AFP/GETTY IMAGES

OZIER MUHAMMAD/NYT

Before introducing the candidate at a rally in Concord, N.H. January 7, 2008.

The campaign used the first night of the Denver convention to carefully reintroduce her with a biopic, "South Side Girl," narrated by her mother, Marian Robinson, in a voice wavering with age. Michelle came across as the all-American girl, carrying an Easter basket and in pigtails, growing up in a close family that embodied the American dream.

The Robinson family lived in a bungalow with "two bedrooms, if you want to be generous," Michelle said. Her father, Fraser Robinson, a city pump operator and Democratic precinct captain, suffered from multiple sclerosis and died in 1991. She doted on him and rarely failed to cite his work ethic and love in her campaign appearances. The Robinsons sent both Michelle and her brother, Craig, to Princeton. Michelle was one of 94 black freshmen in a class of more than 1,100. She roomed with a white student whose mother pleaded with Princeton to give her daughter a white roommate instead. Princeton was followed by Harvard Law, then the white-shoe Chicago firm Sidley & Austin, where Barack Obama arrived as a summer associate in 1989.

He wooed her with ice cream and invitations to hear him speak at community groups. They were married Oct. 18, 1992, in Chicago's Trinity United Church of Christ with the Rev. Jeremiah A. Wright Jr. officiating.

She managed to be the primary breadwinner and, after the girls were born, mother. Known for her 4:30 a.m. treadmill sessions and meals prepared Rachael Ray style, in less than 30 minutes, her friends came up with still another nickname, "The Taskmaster."

In Denver, she returned, time and again, to the theme of family. "I come here as a wife who loves my husband and believes he will be an extraordinary president," she said in her speech. "I come here as a mom whose girls are the heart of my heart and the center of my world. They're the first thing I think about when I wake up in the morning and the last thing I think about when I go to bed at night. Their future and all our children's future is my stake in this election."

Visiting a call center in Akron, Ohio. October 24, 2008.　　　MARK LYONS FOR NYT

Michelle giving Barack a fist bump before he claims the Democratic nomination in St. Paul, Minn. June 3, 2008.

CRAIG LASSIG/EPA

Keynote speech, 2004 Democratic National Convention, Boston. July 27, 2004.

RICHARD PERRY/NYT

Emil Jones made sure to give Obama headline-grabbing issues, including ethics reform and an issue important to the black community, legislation forcing the police to tape interrogations. Obama played in a regular poker game with other legislators.

Still, the legislative footprints he left in Springfield were hardly deep. During the presidential campaign, his record of voting "present" 130 times, rather than casting an aye or a nay, was criticized. And in 1999, he made a rare political miscalculation.

Despite warnings from friends like Newton Minow, he decided to challenge an incumbent Democratic congressman and former Black Panther, Bobby L. Rush. Rush enjoyed deep loyalty in the black community and trounced Obama. "He was blinded by his ambition," Representative Rush said later, but he nonetheless endorsed Obama for president. "Obama has never suffered from a lack of believing that he can accomplish whatever it is he decides to try. Obama believes in Obama. And, frankly, that has its good side but it also has its negative side."

By the time he was sworn into the U.S. Senate, Barack Obama was already a megawatt celebrity.

In 2002, as Washington prepared to wage war in Iraq, Obama contemplated making an antiwar speech, something unusual for a state legislator. He consulted David Axelrod, and gave a speech that managed to carefully thread the political needle. He called the war in Iraq "dumb," while pointing out that he was not opposed to all wars. His early stand against the invasion would give him a defining issue in his run for president.

Unexpectedly, a seat in the U.S. Senate opened up in 2004. This time, Obama was careful to get the blessing of Representative Jesse Jackson Jr., who was thought to have his eye on the seat but had decided against it. The winds were running strongly in Obama's favor. Selected to give the keynote speech at the Democratic convention, he set the place on fire with his youthful energy and lilting rhetoric. Then, his two most serious opponents self-destructed. He won the election with 70 percent of the popular vote.

The new senator from the State of Illinois with his family after his acceptance speech, Chicago. November 2, 2004.

M. SPENCER GREEN/AP

*Barack Obama heads up
the Senate steps to vote on
a bill at the U.S. Capitol.
November 17, 2005.*

By the time he was sworn into the U.S. Senate, Barack Obama was already a megawatt celebrity.

He did not fall in love with Washington. He was 99th in seniority and in the minority party for his first two years. At committee hearings he had to wait to speak until the end.

"I think it is very possible to have a Senate career here that is not particularly useful," he said. He missed his family, especially daughters Malia and Sasha. He and Michelle had decided not to move the family, so Obama commuted between Washington and Chicago, his staff reserving tickets on several flights so that he could be certain to get home to Chicago after the last Senate vote of the week. He was much younger than most of his Senate colleagues and most nights he opted to go to the gym — not the cushy Senate gym but a Chinatown athletic club where he worked out alone.

During the 2006 mid-term elections, Obama was his party's most sought-after campaigner.

Although he won a seat on the coveted Senate Foreign Relations Committee and maintained a solidly liberal voting record, he disappointed some Democrats by not taking a more prominent role in opposing the war. In 2006, he voted against troop withdrawal, arguing that a firm date would hamstring diplomats and military commanders in the field. His most important accomplishment was a push for ethics reform, but as the legislation was reaching the Senate floor, Obama was criticized for not working harder to prevent the bill's collapse.

During the 2006 mid-term elections, Obama was his party's most sought-after campaigner and he raised money for many of his Democratic colleagues. In a matter of days, he raised nearly $1 million online, a glimpse of the fundraising prowess to come.

He was running for president while still getting lost in the Capitol's corridors. ◆

Newly elected Senator Barack Obama with Senior White House Adviser Karl Rove after President George W. Bush's remarks to new members of Congress. January 3, 2005.

With colleague and future running mate Joseph Biden of Delaware during a hearing of the Senate Foreign Relations Committee. April 11, 2005.

Senators Ted Kennedy, Barack Obama and John McCain announce an agreement on procedures for allowing illegal immigrants to apply for citizenship. April 6, 2006.

"A riot nearly broke out when he slipped past his bodyguards at a downtown event and simply smiled at the crowd. 'Obaaammmaaaa!' the people yelled."

—From "Obama Gets a Warm Welcome in Kenya" by Jeffrey Gettleman, The New York Times, August 26, 2006

Senator Barack Obama visits the home of his Kenyan ancestors and addresses a crowd in Nairobi's sprawling Kibera slum. August 27, 2006.

Change I Can Believe In

DAVID BROOKS

I have dreams. I may seem like a boring pundit whose most exotic fantasies involve G.A.O. reports, but deep down, I have dreams. And right now I'm dreaming of the successful presidency this country needs. I'm dreaming of an administration led by Barack Obama, but which stretches beyond the normal Democratic base. It makes time for moderate voters, suburban voters, rural voters and even people who voted for the other guy.

The administration of my dreams understands where the country is today. Its members know that, as Andrew Kohut of the Pew Research Center put it on "The NewsHour," "This was an election where the middle asserted itself." There was "no sign" of a "movement to the left."

Only 17 percent of Americans trust the government to do the right thing most or all of the time, according to an October New York Times/CBS News poll. So the members of my dream Obama administration understand that they cannot impose an ideological program the country does not accept. New presidents in 1932 and 1964 could presuppose a basic level of trust in government. But today, as Bill Galston of the Brookings Institution observes, the new president is going to have to build that trust deliberately and step by step.

Walking into the Obama White House of my dreams will be like walking into the Gates Foundation. The people there will be ostentatiously pragmatic and data-driven. They'll hunt good ideas like venture capitalists. They'll have no faith in all-powerful bureaucrats issuing edicts from the center. Instead, they'll use that language of decentralized networks, bottom-up reform and scalable innovation.

They will actually believe in that stuff Obama says about postpartisan politics. That means there won't just be a few token liberal Republicans in marginal jobs. There will be

people like Robert Gates at Defense and Ray LaHood, Stuart Butler, Diane Ravitch, Douglas Holtz-Eakin and Jim Talent at other important jobs.

The Obama administration of my dreams will insist that Congressional Democrats reinstate bipartisan conference committees. They'll invite G.O.P. leaders to the White House for real meetings and then re-invite them, even if they give hostile press conferences on the White House driveway.

They'll do things conservatives disagree with, but they'll also show that they're not toadies of the liberal interest groups. They'll insist on merit pay and preserving No Child Left Behind's accountability standards, no matter what the teachers' unions say. They'll postpone contentious fights on things like card check legislation.

Most of all, they'll take significant action on the problems facing the country without causing a mass freak-out among voters to the right of Nancy Pelosi.

They'll do this by explaining to the American people that there are two stages to their domestic policy thinking, the short-term and the long-term.

The short-term strategy will have two goals: to mitigate the pain of the recession and to change the culture of Washington. The first step will be to complete the round of stimulus packages that are sure to come.

Then they'll take up two ideas that already have bipartisan support: middle-class tax relief and an energy package. The current economic and energy crisis is an opportunity to do what was not done in similar circumstances in 1974 — transform this country's energy supply. A comprehensive bill — encompassing everything from off-shore drilling to green technologies — would stimulate the economy and nurture new political coalitions.

When the recession shows signs of bottoming out, then

> Walking into the Obama White House of my dreams will be like walking into the Gates Foundation.

KURT KAUPER

my dream administration would begin phase two. The long-term strategy would be about restoring fiscal balances and reforming fundamental institutions.

By this time, the budget deficit could be zooming past $1.5 trillion a year. The U.S. will be borrowing oceans of money from abroad. My dream administration will show that it understands that the remedy for a culture of debt is not more long-term debt. It will side with those who worry that long-term deficits could lead to ruinous interest-rate hikes.

My dream administration will announce a Budget Rebalancing Initiative. Somebody like Representative Jim Cooper would go through the budget and take out the programs and tax expenditures that don't work. "If we have no spending cuts, then we're saying government is perfect. Nobody believes that," Cooper says.

Having built bipartisan relationships, having shown some fiscal toughness, having seen the economy through the tough times, my dream administration will then be in a position to take up health care reform, tax reform, education reform and a long-range infrastructure initiative. These reforms may have to start slow and on the cheap. But real reform would be imaginable since politics as we know it would be transformed.

Is it all just a dream? I hope not. In any case, please be quiet and let me have my moment. ♦

The New York Times, November 7, 2008

A KINDRED SPIRIT

SALLY RYAN FOR NYT

If someone were to rank the long list of people who helped Barack and Michelle Obama get their bearings and build their base in Hyde Park, Valerie Jarrett would be close to the top. Nearly two decades ago, Jarrett swept the young lawyers under her wing, introduced them to a wealthier and better-connected Chicago than their own and eventually secured contacts and money essential to Obama's long-shot Senate victory.

At major campaign speeches, Jarrett would be near the candidate, gazing at him with intensity. Using her intimacy with the Obamas, two BlackBerrys and a cellphone, Jarrett, a real estate executive and civic leader with no national campaign experience, became an internal mediator and external diplomat who secured the trust of black leaders, forged peace with Clintonites and helped talk her old friends through major decisions.

Jarrett, 52, has sometimes been underestimated: perhaps because she is often the only black woman at the boardroom tables where she sits, or perhaps because she can seem girlish, with a pixie haircut, singsong voice and suits that earned her a profile in Vogue.

A protégée of Mayor Richard M. Daley of Chicago, Jarrett served as his planning commissioner, ran a real estate company, the Habitat Company — whose management of public housing projects has come under scrutiny with her rise — and sits on too many boards to count. She is an expert in urban affairs, particularly housing and transportation.

Valerie Bowman was born in Iran in 1956. Her parents had moved there after her father, a physician, was offered less pay in Chicago than his white peers. When the Bowmans tried to teach their young daughter about race, the lessons made no sense to her:

"Like a mom, a big sister, I trust her implicitly," said Michelle Obama.

Valerie, who has light skin, would protest that the Iranians around her had darker skin, so why was she the black one?

When her family returned to Chicago via England, she showed up in public school speaking Farsi, French and English with a British accent. She went on to become a lawyer with degrees from Stanford and the University of Michigan. Her five-year marriage to William R. Jarrett ended in 1988. Dr. Jarrett died in 1991 of a heart attack. Their daughter, Laura, now attends Harvard Law School.

Jarrett met Barack Obama while courting his fiancée, Michelle Robinson, for a job at City Hall, and from that night onward, she was someone with whom the young lawyers could discuss their ambitions. Valerie and Barack bonded over their far-flung childhoods and initial confusion about race. "I wasn't burdened by a personal history of prejudice," she said. "It's part of why I thought Barack could win."

The Obamas were from modest backgrounds, and Jarrett represented the sophistication and intellectual polish of Hyde Park. Her mother, Barbara Bowman, is a child psychologist, and through the generations her family had consistently broken barriers: her great-grandfather was the first black graduate of the Massachusetts Institute of Technology, her father the first black tenured professor in his department at the University of Chicago.

Jarrett is only a few years older than the Obamas, but her relationship with them could seem almost maternal. "I can count on someone like Valerie to take my hand and say, You need to think about these three things," Michelle Obama said. "Like a mom, a big sister, I trust her implicitly."

She was with the Obamas as the election results poured in and her appointment as a senior White House adviser was a foregone conclusion.

President-elect Obama with Valerie Jarrett at Manny's Coffee Shop and Deli in Chicago. November 21, 2008.

KEYNOTE ADDRESS AT THE 2004 DEMOCRATIC CONVENTION

JULY 27, 2004

On behalf of the great state of Illinois, crossroads of a nation, land of Lincoln, let me express my deep gratitude for the privilege of addressing this convention. Tonight is a particular honor for me because, let's face it, my presence on this stage is pretty unlikely. My father was a foreign student, born and raised in a small village in Kenya. He grew up herding goats, went to school in a tin-roof shack. His father, my grandfather, was a cook, a domestic servant.

But my grandfather had larger dreams for his son. Through hard work and perseverance my father got a scholarship to study in a magical place: America, which stood as a beacon of freedom and opportunity to so many who had come before. While studying here, my father met my mother. She was born in a town on the other side of the world, in Kansas. Her father worked on oil rigs and farms through most of the Depression. The day after Pearl Harbor he signed up for duty, joined Patton's army and marched across Europe. Back home, my grandmother raised their baby and went to work on a bomber assembly line. After the war, they studied on the G.I. Bill, bought a house through F.H.A. and moved west in search of opportunity.

And they, too, had big dreams for their daughter, a common dream, born of two continents. My parents shared not only an improbable love; they shared an abiding faith in the possibilities of this nation. They would give me an African name, Barack, or "blessed," believing that in a tolerant America your name is no barrier to success. They imagined me going to the best schools in the land, even though they weren't rich, because in a generous America you don't have to be rich to achieve your potential. They are both passed away now. Yet, I know that on this night they look down on me with pride.

I stand here today, grateful for the diversity of my heritage, aware that my parents' dreams live on in my precious daughters. I stand here knowing that my story is part of the larger American story, that I owe a debt to all of those who came before me, and that in no other country on earth is my story even possible. Tonight we gather to affirm the greatness of our nation, not because of the height of our skyscrapers or the power of our military or the size of our economy. Our pride is based on a very simple premise, summed up in a declaration made over 200 years ago, "We hold these truths to be self-evident, that all men are created equal. That they are endowed by their Creator with certain inalienable rights. That among these are life, liberty and the pursuit of happiness."

That is the true genius of America, a faith in the simple dreams of its people, the insistence on small miracles. That we can tuck in our children at night and know they are fed and clothed and safe from harm. That we can say what we think, write what we think, without hearing a sudden knock on the door. That we can have an idea and start our own business without paying a bribe or hiring somebody's son. That we can participate in the political process without fear of retribution, and that our votes will be counted — or at least, most of the time.

SPENCER PLATT/GETTY IMAGES

This year, in this election, we are called to reaffirm our values and commitments, to hold them against a hard reality and see how we are measuring up to the legacy of our forbearers and the promise of future generations. And fellow Americans — Democrats, Republicans, Independents — I say to you tonight: we have more work to do. More to do for the workers I met in Galesburg, Illinois, who are losing their union jobs at the Maytag plant that's moving to Mexico and now are having to compete with their own children for jobs that pay $7 an hour. More to do for the father I met who was losing his job and choking back tears, wondering how he would pay $4,500 a month for the drugs his son needs without the health benefits he counted on. More to do for the young woman in East St. Louis, and thousands more like her, who has the grades, has the drive, has the will, but doesn't have the money to go to college.

Don't get me wrong. The people I meet in small towns and big cities, in diners and office parks, they don't expect government to solve all their problems. They know they have to work hard to get ahead and they want to. Go into the collar counties around Chicago and people will tell you they don't want their tax money wasted by a welfare agency or the Pentagon. Go into any inner city neighborhood and folks will tell you that government alone can't teach kids to learn. They know that parents have to parent, that children can't achieve unless we raise their expectations and turn off the television sets and eradicate the slander that says a black youth with a book is acting white. No, people don't expect government to solve all their problems. But they sense, deep in their bones, that with just a change in priorities, we can make sure that every child in America has a decent shot at life and that the doors of opportunity remain open to all. They know we can do better. And they want that choice.

In this election, we offer that choice. Our party has chosen a man to lead us who embodies the best this country has to offer. That man is John Kerry. John Kerry understands the ideals of community, faith and sacrifice, because they've defined his life. From his heroic service in Vietnam to his years as prosecutor and lieutenant governor, through two decades in the United States Senate, he has devoted himself to this country. Again and again, we've seen him make tough choices when easier ones were available. His values and his record affirm what is best in us.

John Kerry believes in an America where hard work is rewarded. So instead of offering tax breaks to companies shipping jobs overseas, he'll offer them to companies creating jobs here at home. John Kerry believes in an America where all Americans can afford the same health coverage our politicians in Washington have for themselves. John Kerry believes in energy independence, so we aren't held hostage to the profits of oil companies or the sabotage of foreign oil fields. John Kerry believes in the constitutional freedoms that have made our country the envy of the world, and he will never sacrifice our basic liberties nor use faith as a wedge to divide us. And John Kerry believes that in a dangerous world, war must be an option, but it should never be the first option.

A while back, I met a young man named Shamus at the VFW Hall in East Moline, Illinois. He was a good-looking kid, six-two or six-three, clear-eyed, with an easy smile. He told me he'd joined the Marines and was heading to Iraq the following week. As I listened to him explain why he'd enlisted, his absolute faith in our country and its leaders, his devotion to duty and service, I thought this young man was all any of us might hope for in a child. But then I asked myself: Are we serving Shamus as well as he was serving us? I thought of more than 900 service men and women, sons and daughters, husbands and wives, friends and neighbors, who will not be returning to their hometowns. I thought of families I had met who were struggling to get by without a loved one's full income, or whose loved ones had returned with a limb missing or with nerves shattered, but who still lacked long-term health benefits because they were reservists. When we send our young men and women into harm's way, we have a solemn obligation not to fudge the numbers or shade the truth about why they're going, to care for their families while they're gone, to tend to the soldiers upon their return, and to never ever go to war without enough troops to win the war, secure the peace and earn the respect of the world.

Now let me be clear. We have real enemies in the world. These enemies must be found. They must be pursued and they must be defeated. John Kerry knows this. And just as Lieutenant Kerry did not hesitate to risk his life to protect the men who served with him in Vietnam, President Kerry will not hesitate one moment to use our military might to keep America safe and secure. John Kerry believes in America. And he knows it's not enough for just some of us to prosper. For alongside our famous individualism, there's another ingredient in the American saga.

A belief that we are connected as one people. If there's a child on the south side of Chicago who can't read, that matters to me, even if it's not my child. If there's a senior citizen somewhere who can't pay for her prescription and has to choose between medicine and the rent, that makes my life poorer, even if it's not my grandmother. If there's an Arab-American family being rounded up without benefit of an attorney or due process, that threatens my civil liberties. It's that fundamental belief — I am my brother's keeper, I am my sister's keeper — that makes this country work. It's what allows us to pursue our individual dreams, yet still come together as a single American family. "E pluribus unum." Out of many, one.

Yet even as we speak, there are those who are preparing to divide us, the spin masters and negative ad peddlers who embrace the politics of anything goes. Well, I say to them tonight, there's not a liberal America and a conservative America — there's the United States of America. There's not a black America and white America and Latino America and Asian America; there's the United States of America. The pundits like to slice and dice our country into red states and blue states; red states for Republicans, blue states for Democrats. But I've got news for them, too. We worship an awesome God in the blue states, and we don't like federal agents poking around our libraries in the red states. We coach Little League in the blue states and have gay friends in the red states. There are patriots who opposed the war in Iraq and patriots who supported it. We are one people, all of us pledging allegiance to the stars and stripes, all of us defending the United States of America.

In the end, that's what this election is about. Do we participate in a politics of cynicism or a politics of hope? John Kerry calls on us to hope. John Edwards calls on us to hope. I'm not talking about blind optimism here — the almost willful ignorance that thinks unemployment will go away if we just don't talk about it, or the health care crisis will solve itself if we just ignore it. No, I'm talking about something more substantial. It's the hope of slaves sitting around a fire singing freedom songs; the hope of immigrants setting out for distant shores; the hope of a young naval lieutenant bravely patrolling the Mekong Delta; the hope of a millworker's son who dares to defy the odds; the hope of a skinny kid with a funny name who believes that America has a place for him, too. The audacity of hope!

In the end, that is God's greatest gift to us, the bedrock of this nation; the belief in things not seen; the belief that there are better days ahead. I believe we can give our middle class relief and provide working families with a road to opportunity. I believe we can provide jobs to the jobless, homes to the homeless and reclaim young people in cities across America from violence and despair. I believe that as we stand on the crossroads of history, we can make the right choices, and meet the challenges that face us. America!

Tonight, if you feel the same energy I do, the same urgency I do, the same passion I do, the same hopefulness I do — if we do what we must do, then I have no doubt that all across the country, from Florida to Oregon, from Washington to Maine, the people will rise up in November and John Kerry will be sworn in as president and John Edwards will be sworn in as vice president and this country will reclaim its promise, and out of this long political darkness a brighter day will come. Thank you and God bless you. ♦

There's not a liberal America and a conservative America — there's the United States of America.

Obama and the War on Brains

NICHOLAS D. KRISTOF

Barack Obama's election is a milestone in more than his pigmentation. The second most remarkable thing about his election is that American voters have just picked a president who is an open, out-of-the-closet, practicing intellectual.

Maybe, just maybe, the result will be a step away from the anti-intellectualism that has long been a strain in American life. Smart and educated leadership is no panacea, but we've seen recently that the converse — a White House that scorns expertise and shrugs at nuance — doesn't get very far either.

We can't solve our educational challenges when, according to polls, Americans are approximately as likely to believe in flying saucers as in evolution, and when one-fifth of Americans believe that the sun orbits the Earth.

Almost half of young Americans said in a 2006 poll that it was not necessary to know the locations of countries where important news was made. That must be a relief to Sarah Palin, who, according to Fox News, didn't realize that Africa was a continent rather than a country.

Perhaps John Kennedy was the last president who was unapologetic about his intellect and about luring the best minds to his cabinet. More recently, we've had some smart and well-educated presidents who scrambled to hide it. Richard Nixon was a self-loathing intellectual, and Bill Clinton camouflaged a fulgent brain behind folksy Arkansas aphorisms about hogs.

> Mr. Obama, unlike most politicians near a microphone, exults in complexity.

As for President Bush, he adopted anti-intellectualism as administration policy, repeatedly rejecting expertise (from Middle East experts, climate scientists and reproductive health specialists). Mr. Bush is smart in the sense of remembering facts and faces, yet I can't think of anybody I've ever interviewed who appeared so uninterested in ideas.

At least since Adlai Stevenson's campaigns for the presidency in the 1950s, it's been a disadvantage in American politics to seem too learned. Thoughtfulness is portrayed as wimpishness, and careful deliberation is for sissies. The social critic William Burroughs once bluntly declared that "intellectuals are deviants in the U.S."

(It doesn't help that intellectuals are often as full of themselves as of ideas. After one of Stevenson's high-brow speeches, an admirer yelled out something like, You'll have the vote of every thinking American! Stevenson is said to have shouted back: That's not enough. I need a majority!)

Yet times may be changing. How else do we explain the election in 2008 of an Ivy League–educated law professor who has favorite philosophers and poets?

Granted, Mr. Obama may have been protected from accusations of excessive intelligence by his race. That distracted everyone, and as a black man he didn't fit the stereotype of a pointy-head ivory tower elitist. But it may also be that President Bush has discredited superficiality.

An intellectual is a person interested in ideas and comfortable with complexity. Intellectuals read the classics, even when no one is looking, because they appreciate the lessons of Sophocles and Shakespeare that the world abounds in uncertainties and contradictions, and — President Bush, lend me your ears — that leaders self-destruct when they become too rigid and too intoxicated with the fumes of moral clarity.

(Intellectuals are for real. In contrast, a pedant is a supercilious show-off who drops references to Sophocles and masks his shallowness by using words like "fulgent" and "supercilious.")

Mr. Obama, unlike most politicians near a microphone, exults in complexity. He doesn't condescend or oversimplify nearly as much as politicians often do, and he speaks in paragraphs rather than sound bites. Global Language Monitor, which follows linguistic issues, reports that in the final debate, Mr. Obama spoke at a ninth-grade reading level, while John McCain spoke at a seventh-grade level.

As Mr. Obama prepares to take office, I wish I could say that smart people have a great record in power. They don't. Just think of Emperor Nero, who was one of the most intellectual of ancient rulers — and who also killed his brother, his mother and his pregnant wife; then castrated and married a slave boy who resembled his wife; probably set fire to Rome; and turned Christians into human torches to light his gardens.

James Garfield could simultaneously write Greek with one hand and Latin with the other, Thomas Jefferson was a dazzling scholar and inventor and John Adams typically carried a book of poetry. Yet all were outclassed by George Washington, who was among the least intellectual of our early presidents.

Yet as Mr. Obama goes to Washington, I'm hopeful that his fertile mind will set a new tone for our country. Maybe someday soon our leaders no longer will have to shuffle in shame when they're caught with brains in their heads. ♦

The New York Times, November 9, 2008

CHRISTOPH NIEMANN

RUTH FREMSON/NYT

Senator Barack Obama after formally announcing his run for the presidency, Springfield, Ill. February 10, 2007.

CHAPTER THREE

THE LONG RUN

3

"That is the true genius of America: a faith in the simple dreams of its people; the insistence on small miracles."

JULY 27, 2004

Knocking on doors in Des Moines, Iowa. October 13, 2007.

"He lists the arrows that critics sling his way. He's too hopeful, too inexperienced, not tough enough. At mention of the last, he bobs his head, steps toward the crowd, leans in and says: 'Listen, I'm a black guy named Barack Obama running for president. You want to tell me that I'm not tough enough?'"

—From "On Center Stage, a Candidate Letting His Confidence Show" by Michael Powell, The New York Times, February 24, 2008

RICHARD PERRY/NYT

I T WAS MICHELLE OBAMA WHO KEPT questioning a run for the presidency. She worried about the disruption of their family life and about her husband's safety. Over a Christmas vacation in Hawaii in 2006, the couple visited his grandmother, Toot, and took long walks to talk about Barack's political future. Finally, a decision had to be made and the couple holed up with political consultant David Axelrod, with a few of Obama's lieutenants and trusted friends like Valerie Jarrett.

Michelle wanted assurances on a number of points. Were the Clintons really vulnerable? Would the money be there for a national contest that would drag on for 21 months? And then, after hearing the pros and cons from their six closest political advisers and trusted friends, she turned to her husband.

"You need to ask yourself, Why do you want to do this? What are you hoping to uniquely accomplish, Barack?"

Her husband sat quietly for a moment and then responded: "This I know: When I raise my hand and take that oath of office, I think the world will look at us differently. And millions of kids across this country will look at themselves differently."

A battered America, he believed, was ready for change, ready to live up to its sacred oaths of liberty, justice and equality. President George W. Bush had exhausted and demoralized the country. Going back to the Clinton era wasn't the answer.

Axelrod showed him a set of mock schedules with the states where he would immediately have to start investing time. Obama asked if he would be able to go home on weekends to be with his girls. The answer: not if he wanted to win.

The nucleus of the campaign was a group of Chicago political professionals, Axelrod and one of his younger partners, David Plouffe, who would manage the campaign. Neither man had ever worked on a winning presidential campaign. The core team also included those closest to the Obamas, like Michelle's brother, Craig, a college basketball coach.

The initial campaign plan aimed at dealing Hillary Rodham Clinton, the frontrunner, a devastating blow in the Iowa caucuses in early January. Positioning Clinton as a consummate Washington insider, the strategy called for harnessing the newest technology to

Michelle Obama warms up the crowd for her husband at a fundraising event in New York City. March 9, 2007.

build grassroots enthusiasm, raise record sums of money and build an organization of volunteers across the state. The core theme, from which the campaign never wavered, was change.

An announcement was set for Feb. 10, 2007, a day so frigid that Obama was forced to wear an overcoat and scarf against the cold. He stood before the Old State Capitol in Springfield, Ill., where Abraham Lincoln began his political career, and invoked Lincoln's famous words, "a house divided against itself cannot stand."

In Obama's words, it was the poisoned atmosphere in Washington, a government hobbled by cynicism, petty corruption and "a smallness of our politics," that now divided the nation. "The time for that politics is over," he said. "It is through. It's time to turn the page."

With Michelle now solidly behind the decision to run, he offered a generational call to arms, portraying his campaign less as a candidacy and more as a movement. "Each and every time, a new generation has risen up and done what's needed to be done," he said. "Today we are called once more, and it is time for our generation to answer that call."

He invoked Lincoln's words, "a house divided against itself cannot stand."

One of Obama's aides later asked him how he had prevented his teeth from chattering in the cold. It turned out that a heating device had been positioned at his feet, out of the audience's view.

After an initial burst of interest and enthusiasm following the Springfield announcement, the campaign floundered. In October 2007, Obama told his aides, "Right now we are losing, and we have 90 days to turn it around."

And so they did. Plouffe made good on his pledge to build a first-rate field organization on the ground and opened 37 offices in Iowa. The money came in. Using the Internet to draw in new donors, the campaign hauled in an impressive $24 million during the first quarter of 2007, just behind the Clinton money machine. The campaign, staffed largely by people in their 20s, used Facebook, YouTube and all the power of the Internet to create an ever-widening community of volunteers who could go door to door, serve as precinct captains, raise money and recruit still more

JOSH HANER/NYT

An early Democratic presidential debate in Charleston, S.C. From left, Senator Christopher Dodd of Connecticut, former Senator John Edwards of North Carolina, Senator Hillary Rodham Clinton of New York, Senator Barack Obama of Illinois, Governor Bill Richardson of New Mexico, Senator Joseph R. Biden Jr. of Delaware and Representative Dennis Kucinich of Ohio. July 23, 2007.

"**T**here has been more smoke blown in his direction than anyone in his lifetime, but that's not why he's running,' said former Senator Bob Kerrey, Democrat of Nebraska, who has talked to Mr. Obama in recent weeks. 'He's not lost his reasons for doing this. He realizes that it's his time.'"

—*From "As the Skeptics Ask Why, Obama Asks Why Not?" by Jeff Zeleny, The New York Times, January 18, 2007*

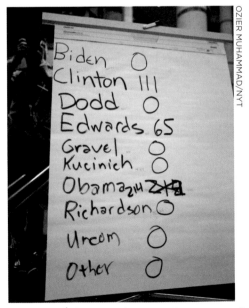

Caucus totals in Des Moines, Iowa. January 3, 2008.

volunteers. Some analysts believed the Web transformed the 2008 election in the same way that television had defined the 1960 contest between Kennedy and Nixon.

Then, using his oratorical talents and story-telling ability to the hilt, Obama brought the house down at the annual Jefferson-Jackson Day dinner in Des Moines, a traditional showcase for the Democratic candidates.

The audience was electrified and some had tears in their eyes as Obama left the stage saying, "Let's go change the world."

One striking anecdote from the speech quickly became a YouTube sensation. In it he recalled a lonely campaign rally in Greenwood, S.C., on a miserable day. Edith Childs, a single voice in the meager crowd, began shouting encouragement. "Fired up! Ready to go!" Soon she had everyone else chanting, too.

Then, pacing back and forth as if marching to the chant, Obama, his voice raised to a spirited shout, asked the crowd, "Are you fired up? Are you ready to go? Fired up! Ready to go!"

The audience was electrified and some had tears in their eyes as Obama left the stage saying, "Let's go change the world."

Hillary Clinton said his liberal message was naïve, his Senate record too scant. He seemed cowed, especially when at one early debate he was waiting to shake her hand and say hello and she turned her back. "Mistress Hillary started disciplining her fellow senator last winter," the Times columnist Maureen Dowd wrote. "When he winked at her, took her elbow and tried to say hello on the Senate floor, she did not melt, as many women do. She brushed him off, a move meant to remind him that he was an upstart who should not get in the way of her turn in the Oval Office."

But it turned out that Iowa Democrats were fired up and ready to go and Hillary had a disappointing third-place finish, behind Obama and second-place finisher John Edwards. It was on to New Hampshire.

Democratic candidates Obama and Clinton during the CNN debate in Los Angeles. January 31, 2008.

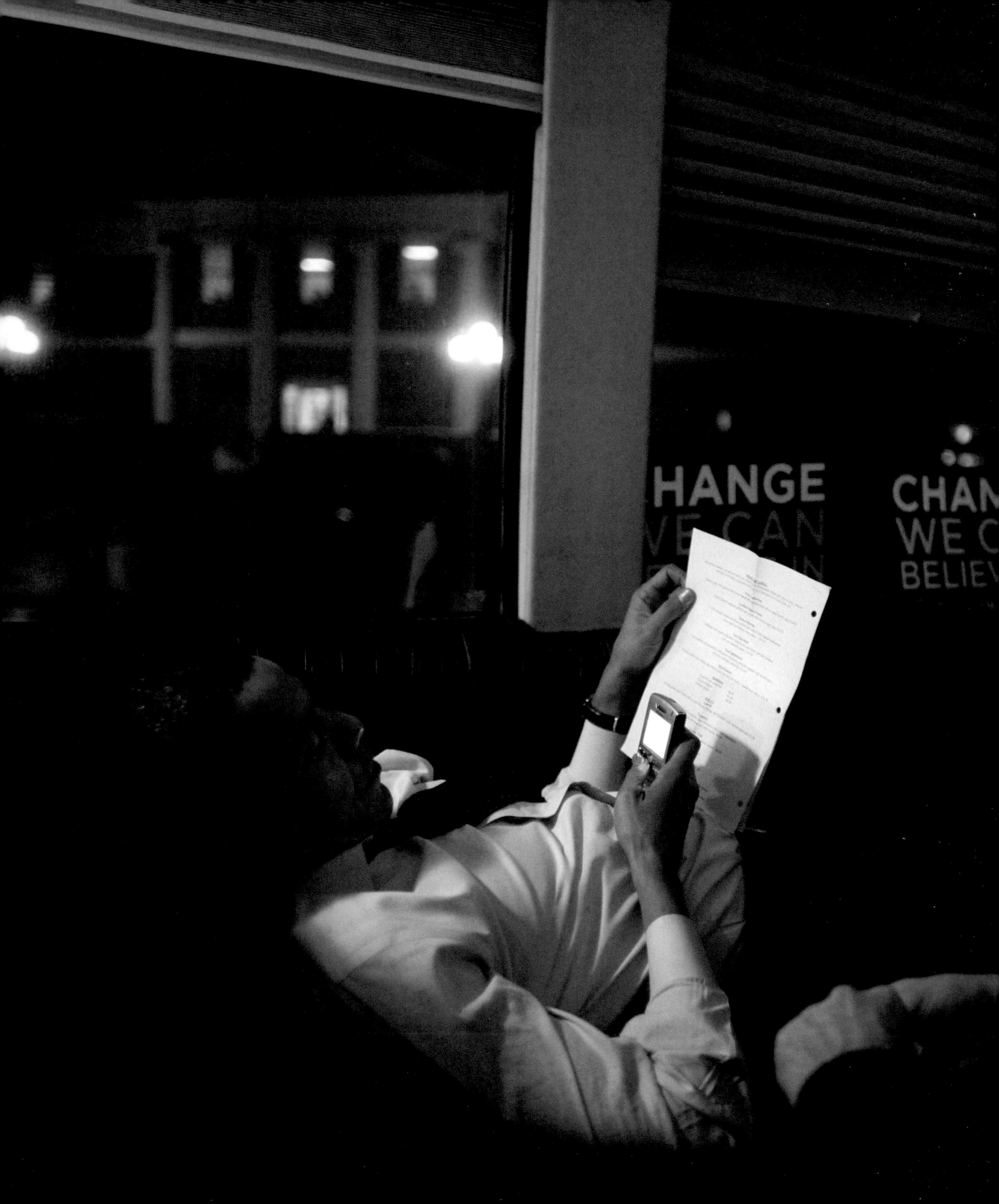
HANGE
VE CAN
CHAN
WE C
BELIEV

Addressing voters in a Manchester theater the Sunday before the primary, Obama was unmistakably a candidate tasting victory. "In two days' time," he intoned, they would be making history. Back-to-back wins in Iowa and New Hampshire, two overwhelmingly white states, would put to rest questions over whether a black candidate could be nominated. But Clinton was able to shed her icy frontrunner persona and even shed tears at a New Hampshire coffee shop, or came close enough. She seemed to find her voice as the heroine of the struggling working class and New Hampshire responded. Obama came in second.

"I guess this is going to go on for awhile," Obama said when aides delivered the disappointing results.

Next came Nevada and then South Carolina, where Bill Clinton, who spent much of the primary season in a red-faced fury over his wife's campaign and especially her treatment by the media (he and others claimed an overt, pro-Obama tilt in the political coverage), made a costly faux pas. The former president, who prided himself on a reputation as the nation's first black president, was accused of playing the race card by comparing the Obama campaign to the narrower appeal of Jesse Jackson. Senator Edward M. Kennedy of Massachusetts, a friend who had taken the Clintons sailing during vacations on Martha's Vineyard, called to protest. Then came another blow to the Clintons when both Kennedy and his niece, Caroline, who had never before endorsed any political candidate outside of her family and up to that point had shown no political ambition, appeared at a Washington, D.C., rally and endorsed Obama. With a huge margin among black voters, he handily won South Carolina.

> *"I guess this is going to go on for awhile," Obama said when aides delivered the disappointing results.*

With North Carolina's John Edwards a perpetual also-ran, Obama and Clinton split states on Super Tuesday. Despite the millions it had raised, the Clinton campaign had not really planned to fight beyond that lollapalooza of primaries. Money was running out and there was internal squabbling among top staffers, problems that bedeviled the campaign through June. Obama's

Aboard the campaign bus with two Obama constants: Chief Strategist David Axelrod and a BlackBerry. January 7, 2008.

"While no polling outfit has systematically canvassed those Americans who are more attuned to the nuances of Hannah Montana than Hannah Arendt, the enthusiasm generated by . . . polls . . . suggests that young children are more engaged in this year's presidential race than any other in recent memory."

—From "Primary Lures Those Too Young to Vote" by Jacques Steinberg,
   The New York Times, April 19, 2008

Shadrick Johnson, 6, was dressed in his Sunday best as he waited to see
Senator Obama in Columbia, S.C. January 20, 2008.

Meeting and greeting at Nicky's Cruisin' Diner, Bangor, Maine. February 9, 2008.

OZIER MUHAMMAD/NYT

team of Axelrod and Plouffe, by contrast, had created a "Feb. 5 and Beyond Room," where money and organization were meticulously allotted to most of the primary and caucus states. Even as Clinton regained momentum in some big states, winning Ohio and Texas, Obama kept pulling out victories in red states and smaller caucus states, building up a steady count in delegates. Money kept flowing in ever-larger streams from the Internet.

The two candidates continued to debate, although the gulf between them on issues was really not that wide. They promised an end to the war in Iraq, more equitable taxation, more effective government spending, more concern for social issues, a restoration of civil liberties and an end to the politics of division of George W. Bush and Karl Rove.

The months of campaigning showed. Obama missed seeing his girls.

Obama and Clinton went out of their way to point out their foreign policy differences, with Clinton portraying herself as a hawkish Democrat and defending her decision to vote in favor of the 2002 resolution that President Bush later considered an authorization to use military force against Saddam Hussein. (Later, she said she fully expected Bush to use diplomacy first — and was shocked that he did not.)

Clinton criticized Obama for being willing to sit down and talk to dictators, including the regime in Iran, although he said he would have a lower-level envoy do preparatory work for a meeting with Iran's leaders first.

On domestic issues, both candidates advocated turning the government onto roughly the same course — shifting resources to help low-income and middle-class Americans, and broadening health coverage dramatically. Clinton criticized Obama's health care plan for not covering all Americans, though her own plan had become less grandiose than the infamous Hillarycare maze of government-paid coverage she had proposed during her husband's first term. She now favored allowing citizens to choose their plans.

Many voters were impressed by Clinton's résumé and her depth of knowledge about America's biggest problems. But Obama built an exciting campaign around the theme of change.

Taking a shot at Riverview High School, Elkhart, Ind. May 4, 2008.

The months of campaigning showed. Obama missed seeing his girls, occasionally railed about having no life and would sometimes lose focus during debates. (His maladroit debate put-down of Hillary as "likable enough" was a typical example.) When Plouffe and Axelrod noticed the fatigue they would dispatch one of the members of the closely knit old crowd from Chicago. Friends like businessman Martin Nesbitt and Dr. Eric Whitaker would then meet up with the candidate and talk him out of the funk. In the presidential campaign, the Obamas had a "no new friends" rule, surrounding themselves with a coterie of familiar faces.

Every primary day, for luck, he played basketball.

"We knew Barack running for president would be hard on him and Michelle, but we didn't realize the impact it would have on us," said Dr. Whitaker, speaking of the frenetic travel schedule he and other friends maintained to keep Obama company.

Clinton, as most candidates do, gained weight on the campaign trail eating too much junk food and the local delicacies proffered by fans. Obama, always preternaturally disciplined, often declined the candy, corndogs and doughnuts pushed his way and most nights ate the same dinner of grilled salmon and broccoli.

"In the final days in Pennsylvania," Maureen Dowd noted in The Times, "he dutifully logged time at diners and force-fed himself waffles, pancakes, sausage and a Philly cheese steak. He split the pancakes with Michelle, left some of the waffle and sausage behind and gave away the French fries that came with the cheese steak." Finally, she wrote, "this is clearly a man who can't wait to get back to his organic scrambled egg whites."

He tried to slip away for frequent workouts in hotel gyms and every primary day, for luck, he played basketball with Reggie Love, 26, his body man, the personal aide who shadows the senator and anticipates everything he needs, from breath mints to tea bags. At 6-foot-5, Love, who played football and basketball at Duke, was about three inches taller than the tall candidate, and fitter.

"There's no doubt that Reggie is cooler than I am," Obama said of his sidekick. "I am living vicariously through Reggie."

An interview on the U.S./Mexico border in Brownsville, Tex. February 29, 2008.

Breakfast at the Glider Diner, Scranton, Pa. April 21, 2008.

There were some missteps. Obama was caught by a blogger describing some white, working-class voters as "bitter." This was a rare verbal stumble for a candidate who was extremely careful with his words and, as a best-selling author, respected their power. Obama used words more fluidly and effectively than any major politician in memory. As a writer he could be lyrical, as a speaker he could be lyrical or crisply matter-of-fact, as the occasion demanded, and he showed uncanny judgment in determining when to be which. Opponents constantly tried to attack him for empty rhetoric, but most of the people who heard him didn't buy that.

But it was the words of Rev. Wright that almost upended his candidacy and pushed Obama to give a speech on race, one that his advisers had warned against. The speech not only saved his campaign but also elevated it.

Going toe to toe with Clinton toughened Obama and made him a better candidate.

In the end, the numbers were the numbers. Clinton kept winning primaries, but Obama's early delegate lead proved insurmountable. It was a long slog, but going toe to toe with Clinton on so many battlegrounds toughened Obama and made him a better candidate. She had previewed all of the arguments the Republicans would launch: he was too eager to deal with rogue dictators; his stands on the issues offered too little substance; most of all, he lacked experience. But he had stood up to her and won. ♦

At a rally in Minneapolis. February 2, 2008.

*The candidate shoots pool at Schultzie's
Billiards in South Charleston, W.V.
May 2008.*

The Obamas (in top two pictures) moments before he claimed the Democratic nomination (bottom picture, on stage). June 3, 2008.

Supporters engulf the nominee in St Paul. June 3, 2008.

"**M**rs. Clinton offered nothing less than a full-throated endorsement for and embrace of Mr. Obama and his candidacy. She has said many times that she would work her heart out for the nominee, and aides said she knew that now was the time to begin to show it."

—From "Ending Her Bid, Clinton Backs Obama" by Adam Nagourney and Jeff Zeleny, The New York Times, June 7, 2008

Senator Hillary Rodham Clinton officially concedes the election, National Building Museum, Washington, D.C. June 7, 2008.

A Father Figure Lost

If his father was a missing presence in Barack Obama's life, another older black man emerged to fill the vacuum: the Rev. Jeremiah A. Wright. In this learned and radical pastor, Obama found a guide who could explain Jesus and faith in terms intellectual no less than emotional, and who helped a man of mixed racial parentage come to understand himself as an African-American.

The two met in the '80s, while Obama was working as a community organizer in Chicago. Wright had built Trinity United Church of Christ into a force, particularly in left-wing politics. With 6,000 members, its congregation was diverse in every way. Wright baptized Obama and sent him off to Harvard Law School with a bag of tapes of his fiery sermons.

Prior to meeting Wright, Obama's religious education had been eclectic, focused more on bits and pieces of different religions and spiritualism that appealed to his mother, who mainly adhered to the tenets of secular humanism. His grandparents were lapsed Baptists and Methodists.

Wright preached black liberation theology, which interprets the Bible as the story of the struggles of black people, who by virtue of their oppression are better able to understand Scripture than those who have suffered less. People flocked to hear his blunt, charismatic preaching, which melded detailed scriptural analysis, black power, Afrocentrism and an emphasis on social justice.

The tightness of the bond between the pastor and his younger disciple was difficult to overstate. The pastor was the first one he thanked when he gained election as a United States senator in 2004. Wright sometimes referred to Obama as his "son." The pastor married the Obamas in 1992, baptized their daughters and blessed their home.

Wright became a central figure in Obama's personal narrative. Obama's embrace of Trinity and its congregants, wealthy and working class and impoverished, formed the climax of his memoir. It was the moment, in his telling, when Obama finally pulled every disparate strand of his background together and found his faith.

In an otherwise meticulous campaign, researchers had neglected to pore over all of Wright's sermons and, in March, some of his most incendiary words, including "God Damn America," were popping up on YouTube.

His grounding in Trinity Church would also bequeath to him a measure of authenticity with the black community, something that helped his credibility as a community organizer and future politician.

At the same time, as he began thinking about a political career, Obama should have been aware that, shorn of their South Side Chicago context, the words and cadences of a politically left-wing black minister could have a very problematic echo.

Just as Barack Obama was hoping to vanquish Hillary Rodham Clinton in a crucial set of spring primaries, the Rev. Jeremiah Wright came roaring into the headlines.

Relations between the preacher, then 66, and his presidential protégé had been strained since Obama's announcement of his candidacy. At the very last minute, Obama had called Wright to cancel his invocation in Springfield, an honor he had every right to expect, as he had blessed every other important event in the Obamas' lives. Campaign aides feared that showcasing Wright would attract controversy and although he came to Springfield to pray with the family just before the announcement, the un-invitation stung. The older man's pride was deeply hurt.

But that was hardly the end of it.

In an otherwise meticulous campaign, researchers had neglected to pore over all of Wright's sermons and, in March, some of his most incendiary words, including "God Damn America," were popping up on YouTube, being cited by conservative talk radio hosts and playing in an endless loop on cable television.

"That was one place where we dropped the ball," said Obama's chief strategist, David Axelrod, his voice growing angry. "The work just wasn't done."

There were clips in which Wright referred to the United States as the "U.S. of K.K.K. A." and said the Sept. 11 attacks were a result of corrupt American foreign policy.

One of the statements that was most replayed came from the sermon Wright had delivered following the Sept. 11 terrorist attacks.

Rev. Jeremiah Wright Jr. at the National Press Club in Washington, D.C. April 28, 2008.

"We have supported state terrorism against the Palestinians and black South Africans, and now we are indignant because the stuff we have done overseas is now brought right back to our own front yards," he said. "America's chickens are coming home to roost."

The minister's defenders tried to explain that the statements were taken out of context, and that he was not antiwhite. Wright's United Church of Christ is majority white and the preacher had given equally scorching lectures about black society, telling audiences to improve their education and work ethic.

The two men rarely, if ever, talked anymore, and Obama increasingly found himself asked to explain and excuse Wright's most elaborate accusations. The controversy reached an apex at the same point Obama seemed to be having particular difficulty winning over white, working class Democrats, pivotal voters in states like Pennsylvania and Ohio, where Clinton was running strong.

Against this backdrop, Obama gave a powerful speech on race. It was a speech some of his advisers opposed, worried that by highlighting race he might exacerbate the suspicions of white primary voters. He chose Philadelphia as the location and wrote every word himself, going out of his way not to include any slogans or phrases that could be pulled out by the press. He wanted the country to absorb the whole thing.

The Philadelphia speech was obviously political, designed to limit the damage that Wright was inflicting on Obama's campaign. But the theme of the speech was broader and more powerful, a call for the country to rise above the use of race as a cynical wedge in the nation's politics. It was an appeal to fair-minded Americans, regardless of whether they supported Obama for president.

The speech was only obliquely about Wright, about whom Obama said, "As imperfect as he may be, he has been like family to me," adding: "He strengthened my faith, officiated my wedding and baptized my children. Not once in my conversations with him have I heard him talk about any ethnic group in derogatory terms."

That might have ended the story, but Wright was not mollified. He gave more interviews and a clownish speech at the National Press Club in Washington, D.C., where he continued his more outrageous rants. After several more days of progressive distancing, Obama closeted himself with some of the pastor's recent speeches and watched some of the footage. With an obviously pained heart, he finally cut all ties and announced that he and his family were leaving Trinity United.

BARRY BLITT

A President Like My Father

CAROLINE KENNEDY

OVER THE YEARS, I've been deeply moved by the people who've told me they wished they could feel inspired and hopeful about America the way people did when my father was president. This sense is even more profound today. That is why I am supporting a presidential candidate in the Democratic primaries, Barack Obama.

My reasons are patriotic, political and personal, and the three are intertwined. All my life, people have told me that my father changed their lives, that they got involved in public service or politics because he asked them to. And the generation he inspired has passed that spirit on to its children. I meet young people who were born long after John F. Kennedy was president, yet who ask me how to live out his ideals.

Sometimes it takes a while to recognize that someone has a special ability to get us to believe in ourselves, to tie that belief to our highest ideals and imagine that together we can do great things. In those rare moments, when such a person comes along, we need to put aside our plans and reach for what we know is possible.

We have that kind of opportunity with Senator Obama. It isn't that the other candidates are not experienced or knowledgeable. But this year, that may not be enough. We need a change in the leadership of this country — just as we did in 1960.

Most of us would prefer to base our voting decision on policy differences. However, the candidates' goals are similar. They have all laid out detailed plans on everything from strengthening our middle class to investing in early childhood education. So qualities of leadership, character and judgment play a larger role than usual.

Senator Obama has demonstrated these qualities throughout his more than two decades of public service, not just in the United States Senate but in Illinois, where he helped turn around struggling communities, taught constitutional law and was an elected state official for eight years. And Senator Obama is showing the same qualities today. He has built a movement that is changing the face of politics in this country, and he has demonstrated a special gift for inspiring young people — known for a willingness to volunteer, but an aversion to politics — to become engaged in the political process.

I have spent the past five years working in the New York City public schools and have three teenage children of my own. There is a generation coming of age that is hopeful, hard-working, innovative and imaginative. But too many of them are also hopeless, defeated and disengaged. As parents, we have a responsibility to help our children to believe in themselves and in their power to shape their future. Senator Obama is inspiring my children, my parents' grandchildren, with that sense of possibility.

Senator Obama is running a dignified and honest campaign. He has spoken eloquently about the role of faith in his life, and opened a window into his character in two compelling books. And when it comes to judgment, Barack Obama made the right call on the most important issue of our time by opposing the war in Iraq from the beginning.

I want a president who understands that his responsibility is to articulate a vision and encourage others to achieve it; who holds himself, and those around him, to the highest ethical standards; who appeals to the hopes of those who still believe in the American Dream, and those around the world who still believe in the American ideal; and who can lift our spirits, and make us believe again that our country needs every one of us to get involved.

I have never had a president who inspired me the way people tell me that my father inspired them. But for the first time, I believe I have found the man who could be that president — not just for me, but for a new generation of Americans. ◆

> My reasons are patriotic, political and personal, and the three are intertwined.

The New York Times, January 27, 2008

A More Perfect Union

MARCH 18, 2008

"We the people, in order to form a more perfect union."

Two hundred and twenty one years ago, in a hall that still stands across the street, a group of men gathered and, with these simple words, launched America's improbable experiment in democracy. Farmers and scholars; statesmen and patriots who had traveled across an ocean to escape tyranny and persecution finally made real their declaration of independence at a Philadelphia convention that lasted through the spring of 1787.

The document they produced was eventually signed but ultimately unfinished. It was stained by this nation's original sin of slavery, a question that divided the colonies and brought the convention to a stalemate until the founders chose to allow the slave trade to continue for at least 20 more years, and to leave any final resolution to future generations.

Of course, the answer to the slavery question was already embedded within our Constitution — a Constitution that had at its very core the ideal of equal citizenship under the law; a Constitution that promised its people liberty, and justice, and a union that could be and should be perfected over time.

And yet words on a parchment would not be enough to deliver slaves from bondage, or provide men and women of every color and creed their full rights and obligations as citizens of the United States. What would be needed were Americans in successive generations who were willing to do their part — through protests and struggle, on the streets and in the courts, through a civil war and civil disobedience and always at great risk — to narrow that gap between the promise of our ideals and the reality of their time.

This was one of the tasks we set forth at the beginning of this campaign — to continue the long march of those who came before us, a march for a more just, more equal, more free, more caring and more prosperous America. I chose to run for the presidency at this moment in history because I believe deeply that we cannot solve the challenges of our time unless we solve them together — unless we perfect our union by understanding that we may have different stories, but we hold common hopes; that we may not look the same and we may not have come from the same place, but we all want to move in the same direction — towards a better future for our children and our grandchildren.

This belief comes from my unyielding faith in the decency and generosity of the American people. But it also comes from my own American story.

JESSICA KOURKOUNIS FOR NYT

I am the son of a black man from Kenya and a white woman from Kansas. I was raised with the help of a white grandfather who survived a Depression to serve in Patton's Army during World War II and a white grandmother who worked on a bomber assembly line at Fort Leavenworth while he was overseas. I've gone to some of the best schools in America and lived in one of the world's poorest nations. I am married to a black American who carries within her the blood of slaves and slaveowners — an inheritance we pass on to our two precious daughters. I have brothers, sisters, nieces, nephews, uncles and cousins, of every race and every hue, scattered across three continents, and for as long as I live, I will never forget that in no other country on Earth is my story even possible.

It's a story that hasn't made me the most conventional candidate. But it is a story that has seared into my genetic makeup the idea that this nation is more than the sum of its parts — that out of many, we are truly one.

Throughout the first year of this campaign, against all predictions to the contrary, we saw how hungry the American people were for this message of unity. Despite the temptation to view my candidacy through a purely racial lens, we won commanding victories in states with some of the whitest populations in the country. In South Carolina, where the Confederate Flag still flies, we built a powerful coalition of African Americans and white Americans.

This is not to say that race has not been an issue in the campaign. At various stages in the campaign, some commentators have deemed me either "too black" or "not black enough." We saw racial tensions bubble to the surface during the week before the South Carolina primary. The press has scoured every exit poll for the latest evidence of racial polarization, not just in terms of white and black, but black and brown as well.

And yet, it has only been in the last couple of weeks that the discussion of race in this campaign has taken a particularly divisive turn.

On one end of the spectrum, we've heard the implication that my candidacy is somehow an exercise in affirmative action; that it's based solely on the desire of wide-eyed liberals to purchase racial reconciliation on the cheap. On the other end, we've heard my former pastor, Reverend Jeremiah Wright, use incendiary language to express views that have the potential not only to widen the racial divide, but views that denigrate both the greatness and the goodness of our nation; that rightly offend white and black alike.

I have already condemned, in unequivocal terms, the statements of Reverend Wright that have caused such controversy. For some, nagging questions remain. Did I know him to be an occasionally fierce critic of American domestic and foreign policy? Of course. Did I ever hear him make remarks that could be considered controversial while I sat in church? Yes. Did I strongly disagree with many of his political views? Absolutely — just as I'm sure many of you have heard remarks from your pastors, priests, or rabbis with which you strongly disagreed.

But the remarks that have caused this recent firestorm weren't simply controversial. They weren't simply a religious leader's effort to speak out against perceived injustice. Instead, they expressed a profoundly distorted view of this country — a view that sees white racism as endemic, and that elevates what is wrong with America above all that we know is right with America; a view that sees the conflicts in the Middle East as rooted primarily in the actions of stalwart allies like Israel, instead of emanating from the perverse and hateful ideologies of radical Islam.

As such, Reverend Wright's comments were not only wrong but divisive, divisive at a time when we need unity; racially charged at a time when we need to come together to solve a set of monumental problems — two wars, a terrorist threat, a falling economy, a chronic health care crisis and potentially devastating climate change; problems that are neither black or white or Latino or Asian, but rather problems that confront us all.

Given my background, my politics, and my professed values

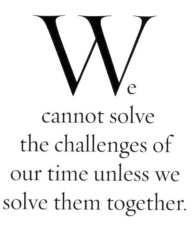

We cannot solve the challenges of our time unless we solve them together.

and ideals, there will no doubt be those for whom my statements of condemnation are not enough. Why associate myself with Reverend Wright in the first place, they may ask? Why not join another church? And I confess that if all that I knew of Reverend Wright were the snippets of those sermons that have run in an endless loop on the television and YouTube, or if Trinity United Church of Christ conformed to the caricatures being peddled by some commentators, there is no doubt that I would react in much the same way.

But the truth is, that isn't all that I know of the man. The man I met more than 20 years ago is a man who helped introduce me to my Christian faith, a man who spoke to me about our obligations to love one another; to care for the sick and lift up the poor. He is a man who served his country as a U.S. Marine; who has studied and lectured at some of the finest universities and seminaries in the country, and who for over 30 years led a church that serves the community by doing God's work here on Earth — by housing the homeless, ministering to the needy, providing day care services and scholarships and prison ministries, and reaching out to those suffering from HIV/AIDS.

In my first book, "Dreams From My Father," I described the experience of my first service at Trinity:

"People began to shout, to rise from their seats and clap and cry out, a forceful wind carrying the reverend's voice up into the rafters. . . . And in that single note — hope! — I heard something else; at the foot of that cross, inside the thousands of churches across the city, I imagined the stories of ordinary black people merging with the stories of David and Goliath, Moses and Pharaoh, the Christians in the lion's den, Ezekiel's field of dry bones. Those stories — of survival, and freedom, and hope — became our story, my story; the blood that had spilled was our blood, the tears our tears; until this black church, on this bright day, seemed once more a vessel carrying the story of a people into future generations and into a larger world. Our trials and triumphs became at once unique and universal, black and more than black; in chronicling our journey, the stories and songs gave us a means to reclaim memories that we didn't need to feel shame about . . . memories that all people might study and cherish — and with which we could start to rebuild."

A MORE PERFECT UNION
MARCH 18, 2008

That has been my experience at Trinity. Like other predominantly black churches across the country, Trinity embodies the black community in its entirety — the doctor and the welfare mom, the model student and the former gang-banger. Like other black churches, Trinity's services are full of raucous laughter and sometimes bawdy humor. They are full of dancing, clapping, screaming and shouting that may seem jarring to the untrained ear. The church contains in full the kindness and cruelty, the fierce intelligence and the shocking ignorance, the struggles and successes, the love and yes, the bitterness and bias that make up the black experience in America.

And this helps explain, perhaps, my relationship with Reverend Wright. As imperfect as he may be, he has been like family to me. He strengthened my faith, officiated my wedding and baptized my children. Not once in my conversations with him have I heard him talk about any ethnic group in derogatory terms, or treat whites with whom he interacted with anything but courtesy and respect. He contains within him the contradictions — the good and the bad — of the community that he has served diligently for so many years.

I can no more disown him than I can disown the black community. I can no more disown him than I can my white grandmother — a woman who helped raise me, a woman who sacrificed again and again for me, a woman who loves me as much as she loves anything in this world, but a woman who once confessed her fear of black men who passed by her on the street, and who on more than one occasion has uttered racial or ethnic stereotypes that made me cringe.

These people are a part of me. And they are a part of America, this country that I love.

Some will see this as an attempt to justify or excuse comments that are simply inexcusable. I can assure you it is not. I suppose the politically safe thing would be to move on from this episode and just hope that it fades into the woodwork. We can dismiss Reverend Wright as a crank or a demagogue, just as some have dismissed Geraldine Ferraro, in the aftermath of her recent statements, as harboring some deep-seated racial bias.

But race is an issue that I believe this nation cannot afford to ignore right now. We would be making the same mistake that Reverend Wright made in his offending sermons about America — to simplify and stereotype and amplify the negative to the point that it distorts reality.

The fact is that the comments that have been made and the issues that have surfaced over the last few weeks reflect the complexities of race in this country that we've never really worked through — a part of our union that we have yet to perfect. And if we walk away now, if we simply retreat into our respective corners, we will never be able to come together and solve challenges like health care, or education, or the need to find good jobs for every American.

Understanding this reality requires a reminder of how we arrived at this point. As William Faulkner once wrote, "The past isn't dead and buried. In fact, it isn't even past." We do not need to recite here the history of racial injustice in this country. But we do need to remind ourselves that so many of the disparities that exist in the African-American community today can be directly traced to inequalities passed on from an earlier generation that suffered under the brutal legacy of slavery and Jim Crow.

Segregated schools were, and are, inferior schools; we still haven't fixed them, 50 years after Brown v. Board of Education, and the inferior education they provided, then and now, helps explain the pervasive achievement gap between today's black and white students.

Legalized discrimination — where blacks were prevented, often through violence, from owning property, or loans were not granted to African-American business owners, or black homeowners could not access FHA mortgages, or blacks were excluded from unions, or the police force, or fire departments — meant that black families could not amass any meaningful wealth to bequeath to future generations. That history helps explain the wealth and income gap between black and white, and the concentrated pockets of poverty that persists in so many of today's urban and rural communities.

A lack of economic opportunity among black men, and the shame and frustration that came from not being able to provide for one's family, contributed to the erosion of black families — a problem that welfare policies for many years may have worsened. And the lack of basic services in so many urban black neighborhoods — parks for kids to play in, police walking the beat, regular garbage pick-up and building code enforcement — all helped create a cycle

> **R**ace is an issue that I believe this nation cannot afford to ignore right now.

of violence, blight and neglect that continue to haunt us.

This is the reality in which Reverend Wright and other African-Americans of his generation grew up. They came of age in the late 50's and early 60's, a time when segregation was still the law of the land and opportunity was systematically constricted. What's remarkable is not how many failed in the face of discrimination, but rather how many men and women overcame the odds; how many were able to make a way out of no way for those like me who would come after them.

But for all those who scratched and clawed their way to get a piece of the American Dream, there were many who didn't make it — those who were ultimately defeated, in one way or another, by discrimination. That legacy of defeat was passed on to future generations — those young men and increasingly young women who we see standing on street corners or languishing in our prisons, without hope or prospects for the future. Even for those blacks who did make it, questions of race, and racism, continue to define their worldview in fundamental ways. For the men and women of Reverend Wright's generation, the memories of humiliation and doubt and fear have not gone away; nor have the anger and the bitterness of those years. That anger may not get expressed in public, in front of white co-workers or white friends. But it does find voice in the barbershop or around the kitchen table. At times, that anger is exploited by politicians, to gin up votes along racial lines, or to make up for a politician's own failings.

JESSICA KOURKOUNIS FOR NYT

And occasionally it finds voice in the church on Sunday morning, in the pulpit and in the pews. The fact that so many people are surprised to hear that anger in some of Reverend Wright's sermons simply reminds us of the old truism that the most segregated hour in American life occurs on Sunday morning. That anger is not always productive; indeed, all too often it distracts attention from solving real problems; it keeps us from squarely facing our own complicity in our condition, and prevents the African-American community from forging the alliances it needs to bring about real change. But the anger is real; it is powerful; and to simply wish it away, to condemn it without understanding its roots, only serves to widen the chasm of misunderstanding that exists between the races.

In fact, a similar anger exists within segments of the white community. Most working- and middle-class white Americans don't feel that they have been particularly privileged by their race. Their experience is the immigrant experience — as far as they're concerned, no one's handed them anything, they've built it from scratch. They've worked hard all their lives, many times only to see their jobs shipped overseas or their pension dumped after a lifetime of labor. They are anxious about their futures, and feel their dreams slipping away; in an era of stagnant wages and global competition, opportunity comes to be seen as a zero-sum game, in which your dreams come at my expense. So when they are told to bus their children to a school across town; when they hear that an African American is getting an advantage in landing a good job or a spot in a good college because of an injustice that they themselves never committed; when they're told that their fears about crime in urban neighborhoods are somehow prejudiced, resentment builds over time.

Like the anger within the black community, these resentments aren't always expressed in polite company. But they have helped shape the political landscape for at least a generation. Anger over welfare and affirmative action helped forge the Reagan Coalition. Politicians routinely exploited fears of crime for their own electoral ends. Talk show hosts and conservative commentators built entire careers unmasking bogus claims of racism while dismissing legitimate discussions of racial injustice and inequality as mere political correctness or reverse racism.

Just as black anger often proved counterproductive, so have these white resentments distracted attention from the real culprits of the middle-class squeeze — a corporate culture rife with inside dealing, questionable accounting practices and short-term greed; a Washington dominated by lobbyists and special interests; economic policies that favor the few over the many. And yet, to wish away the resentments of white Americans, to label them as misguided or even racist, without recognizing they are grounded in legitimate concerns — this too widens the racial divide, and blocks the path to understanding.

This is where we are right now. It's a racial stalemate we've been stuck in for years. Contrary to the claims of some of my critics, black and white, I have never been so naïve as to believe that we can get beyond our racial divisions in a single election cycle, or with a single candidacy — particularly a candidacy as imperfect as my own.

A More Perfect Union
MARCH 18, 2008

But I have asserted a firm conviction — a conviction rooted in my faith in God and my faith in the American people — that working together we can move beyond some of our old racial wounds, and that in fact we have no choice if we are to continue on the path of a more perfect union.

For the African-American community, that path means embracing the burdens of our past without becoming victims of our past. It means continuing to insist on a full measure of justice in every aspect of American life. But it also means binding our particular grievances — for better health care, and better schools and better jobs — to the larger aspirations of all Americans — the white woman struggling to break the glass ceiling, the white man who's been laid off, the immigrant trying to feed his family. And it means taking full responsibility for own lives — by demanding more from our fathers, and spending more time with our children, and reading to them and teaching them that while they may face challenges and discrimination in their own lives, they must never succumb to despair or cynicism; they must always believe that they can write their own destiny.

Ironically, this quintessentially American — and, yes, conservative — notion of self-help found frequent expression in Reverend Wright's sermons. But what my former pastor too often failed to understand is that embarking on a program of self-help also requires a belief that society can change.

The profound mistake of Reverend Wright's sermons is not that he spoke about racism in our society. It's that he spoke as if our society was static; as if no progress has been made; as if this country — a country that has made it possible for one of his own members to run for the highest office in the land and build a coalition of white and black, Latino and Asian, rich and poor, young and old — is still irrevocably bound to a tragic past. But what we know — what we have seen — is that America can change. That is the true genius of this nation. What we have already achieved gives us hope — the audacity to hope — for what we can and must achieve tomorrow.

In the white community, the path to a more perfect union means acknowledging that what ails the African-American community does not just exist in the minds of black people; that the legacy of discrimination — and current incidents of discrimina-

tion, while less overt than in the past — are real and must be addressed. Not just with words, but with deeds — by investing in our schools and our communities; by enforcing our civil rights laws and ensuring fairness in our criminal justice system; by providing this generation with ladders of opportunity that were unavailable for previous generations. It requires all Americans to realize that your dreams do not have to come at the expense of my dreams; that investing in the health, welfare, and education of black and brown and white children will ultimately help all of America prosper.

In the end, then, what is called for is nothing more, and nothing less, than what all the world's great religions demand — that we do unto others as we would have them do unto us. Let us be our brother's keeper, Scripture tells us. Let us be our sister's keeper. Let us find that common stake we all have in one another, and let our politics reflect that spirit as well.

For we have a choice in this country. We can accept a politics that breeds division, and conflict and cynicism. We can tackle race only as spectacle — as we did in the O.J. trial — or in the wake of tragedy, as we did in the aftermath of Katrina — or as fodder for the nightly news. We can play Reverend Wright's sermons on every channel, every day and talk about them from now until the election, and make the only question in this campaign whether or not the American people think that I somehow believe or sympathize with his most offensive words. We can pounce on some gaffe by a Hillary supporter as evidence that she's playing the race card, or we can speculate on whether white men will all flock to John McCain in the general election regardless of his policies.

We can do that.

But if we do, I can tell you that in the next election, we'll be talking about some other distraction. And then another one. And then another one. And nothing will change.

That is one option. Or, at this moment, in this election, we can come together and say, "Not this time." This time we want to talk about the crumbling schools that are stealing the future of black children and white children and Asian children and Hispanic children and Native American children. This time we want to reject the cynicism that tells us that these kids can't learn; that those kids who don't look like us are somebody else's problem.

> **W**orking together we can move beyond some of our old racial wounds.

The children of America are not those kids, they are our kids, and we will not let them fall behind in a 21st-century economy. Not this time.

This time we want to talk about how the lines in the emergency room are filled with whites and blacks and Hispanics who do not have health care; who don't have the power on their own to overcome the special interests in Washington, but who can take them on if we do it together.

This time we want to talk about the shuttered mills that once provided a decent life for men and women of every race, and the homes for sale that once belonged to Americans from every religion, every region, every walk of life. This time we want to talk about the fact that the real problem is not that someone who doesn't look like you might take your job; it's that the corporation you work for will ship it overseas for nothing more than a profit.

This time we want to talk about the men and women of every color and creed who serve together, and fight together and bleed together under the same proud flag. We want to talk about how to bring them home from a war that never should've been authorized and never should've been waged, and we want to talk about how we'll show our patriotism by caring for them, and their families, and giving them the benefits they have earned.

I would not be running for president if I didn't believe with all my heart that this is what the vast majority of Americans want for this country. This union may never be perfect, but generation after generation has shown that it can always be perfected. And today, whenever I find myself feeling doubtful or cynical about this possibility, what gives me the most hope is the next generation — the young people whose attitudes and beliefs and openness to change have already made history in this election.

There is one story in particular that I'd like to leave you with today — a story I told when I had the great honor of speaking on Dr. King's birthday at his home church, Ebenezer Baptist, in Atlanta.

There is a young, twenty-three-year-old white woman named Ashley Baia who organized for our campaign in Florence, South Carolina. She had been working to organize a mostly African-American community since the beginning of this campaign, and one day she was at a roundtable discussion where everyone went around telling their story and why they were there.

And Ashley said that when she was nine years old, her mother got cancer. And because she had to miss days of work, she was let go and lost her health care. They had to file for bankruptcy, and that's when Ashley decided that she had to do something to help her mom.

She knew that food was one of their most expensive costs, and so Ashley convinced her mother that what she really liked and really wanted to eat more than anything else was mustard and relish sandwiches. Because that was the cheapest way to eat.

She did this for a year until her mom got better, and she told everyone at the roundtable that the reason she joined our campaign was so that she could help the millions of other children in the country who want and need to help their parents too.

Now Ashley might have made a different choice. Perhaps somebody told her along the way that the source of her mother's problems were blacks who were on welfare and too lazy to work, or Hispanics who were coming into the country illegally. But she didn't. She sought out allies in her fight against injustice.

Anyway, Ashley finishes her story and then goes around the room and asks everyone else why they're supporting the campaign. They all have different stories and reasons. Many bring up a specific issue. And finally they come to this elderly black man who's been sitting there quietly the entire time. And Ashley asks him why he's there. And he does not bring up a specific issue. He does not say health care or the economy. He does not say education or the war. He does not say that he was there because of Barack Obama. He simply says to everyone in the room, "I am here because of Ashley."

"I'm here because of Ashley." By itself, that single moment of recognition between that young white girl and that old black man is not enough. It is not enough to give health care to the sick, or jobs to the jobless, or education to our children.

But it is where we start. It is where our union grows stronger. And as so many generations have come to realize over the course of the 221 years since a band of patriots signed that document in Philadelphia, that is where the perfection begins. ♦

> This union may never be perfect, but generation after generation has shown that it can always be perfected.

PHILIP BURKE

Commentary

Yes You Can!

FRANK RICH

Long before it became the triumphant political buzzword of our new century, change was the idea that animated America. Go West, reinvent yourself, pick yourself up, keep moving, don't look back: Such were the cultural imperatives that built a nation, driving a wildly heterogeneous people to imagine a new world in which freedom upended the stale hierarchies of the old. The corollary American ideal was no less monumental, but too often honored more in theory than in practice: All men are created equal.

In 2008 the idea and the ideal converged in the remarkable ascension of Barack Obama.

That Obama is the first black man to win America's highest office is the inspiring headline on the story, but hardly the whole tale. The son of a father from Kenya and a white mother from heartland Kansas, he is, as he has humorously put it, "a mutt," embodying not just America's racial mix but also its polyglot immigrant roots. Raised mainly in Hawaii, he is also a product of the most remote outpost of the American frontier. And yet he sought an education in the effete Ivy League bastions of the East before settling in Chicago, the least rarefied of all American cities, where urbanity is always tempered by the hard-knuckled realism and outright brawn that powered the nation's industrial past.

This crazy-quilt background made Obama a long-shot candidate for president. What's more, at age 47, Obama had a résumé nearly as slender as his political opponents said it was. His principal 2008 political adversaries, Hillary Rodham Clinton and John McCain, were far better known quantities, paragons of Washington experience.

At a time of two wars and growing economic panic, it would hardly seem logical that American voters would pass over these brand names for a young man few had even heard of before he delivered his first speech on national television at the Democratic National Convention in 2004.

That they did is a testament both to the man and to the country. Obama illuminated his potential as the nation's chief executive by getting the job done in a marathon campaign, running an organization that took on the toughest machine in Democratic politics without flinching and that never wavered from its message even when his candidacy hit its inevitable potholes. That message was not just of change but of an inclusive approach to governance, a direct byproduct of his experience as a community organizer. Obama wasn't merely preaching some sentimental, Kumbaya-style homily of American unity, as some critics would have it, but enacting it day by day in a campaign that was determined to enlist all ages, races and states as well as both political parties. He illustrated his style of leadership on the fly, in real time.

Obama's calm under fire appealed to Americans reeling in tough times. So did his manifest decency and thoughtfulness. But equally significant was Obama's ability to make Americans see themselves in a better light. In the years since 9/11, fear has been the most common currency of our politics. Fear of terrorism has been exploited by leaders to whip up fear of new ideas, fear of new people, fear of anyone who looks different or even bears a foreign-sounding name.

For much of 2008, Obama's opponents and much of the press assumed that Americans would remain too fearful to ever vote for a black man named Barack Hussein Obama even if he seemed the most qualified for the Herculean job at hand. But in defiance of those expectations, Americans said yes, they could — and did. In the profound privacy of the voting booth, they put aside old fears, turned out an old order and reinvented their country once again. Now the world waits, with high hopes, for this unlikely new president to vindicate his fellow citizens' reawakened faith in America's eternal capacity for change. ◆

> That Obama is the first black man to win America's highest office is the inspiring headline on the story, but hardly the whole tale.

Barack Obama boarding his plane in Indianapolis for a flight to Hawaii to visit his ailing grandmother. October 23, 2008.

CHAPTER FOUR

THE RACE TO THE WHITE HOUSE

"There's a certain tone in politics I aspire to that allows me to disagree with people without being disagreeable."

JUNE 4, 2004

WHILE BARACK OBAMA PROJECTED youth and change, John McCain, the Republican nominee who turned 72 during the campaign, was running on his distinguished biography and experience. A former POW in Vietnam, the Arizona senator was admired for his straight talk and independent stands on contentious issues, such as torture of detainees, campaign finance and immigration reform. And he should have enjoyed one tremendous advantage.

After a decisive win in New Hampshire, he had wrapped up his party's nomination in early March, leaving Obama and Hillary Rodham Clinton to slug it out over a long, divisive spring.

But McCain found himself tethered to an unpopular incumbent president, George W. Bush, and an even more unpopular war. McCain not only supported the war in Iraq, he insisted the United States was winning it. Obama, of course, had promised to end it.

As it turned out, though, national security was not the dominant issue. All spring and summer, the economy had faltered. By the fall, the bursting housing bubble had become a four-alarm financial crisis, requiring an emergency federal bailout of the country's leading financial institutions. The political environment for Republicans went from challenging to downright sour.

The mood at Obama's headquarters on Chicago's Michigan Avenue was anything but. The office was jammed with young aides, pizza boxes and the latest technology. Campaign contributions were pouring in. Some of the Clintonites, including Hillary Clinton's former campaign manager, had moved in to work for Obama. On the stump, McCain often looked every one of his 70-plus years. The conservative base of the G.O.P. still suspected him of being a Republican in name only.

Senator McCain at a rally in Columbus, Ohio. October 31, 2008.

"When McCain reaches for a pop culture reference, it is for the Beach Boys' 'Barbara Ann.' Mr. Obama drops casual references to Jay-Z."

—From "Age Becomes the New Race and Gender" by Adam Nagourney, The New York Times, June 15, 2008

Preparing to board the campaign plane, Columbus, Ohio. November 2, 2008.

Senator Obama at the Western Wall in Jerusalem during his overseas trip. July 24, 2008.

The only strategy that seemed to make a win possible under such circumstances was to go heavily negative against Obama, but McCain saw himself as a man of honor. In 2000, he had run a rollicking campaign for the White House, touring the country in a bus called "The Straight Talk Express," and inviting reporters and friends to ride alongside. But in a bitter primary showdown in South Carolina, he had lost to George W. Bush. For his 2008 campaign McCain hired many members of the Bush political team. When he protested their negative, hardball tactics, they reminded him of that loss. They closeted the candidate from the press. McCain seemed to grow cranky and frustrated.

The McCain team began airing an attack ad portraying [Obama] as "the biggest celebrity in the world."

In late July, Obama toured the Middle East and Europe on a trip intended to make him appear presidential, but the trip also showcased him as a political rock star. The McCain campaign pounced. After Obama appeared before a huge crowd at the Brandenburg Gate in Berlin, the McCain team began airing an attack ad portraying him as "the biggest celebrity in the world," juxtaposing the Berlin speech with pictures of Britney Spears and Paris Hilton.

Money helped insulate the Obama campaign from the attacks. The candidate had made a fateful decision to forgo $84 million in federal election funds for the general election in order to raise donations outside of the limits of the Watergate-era campaign finance strictures. The campaign ended up raising $750 million, more than George W. Bush and John Kerry combined had raised in 2004 and hundreds of millions more than McCain. McCain, who made campaign finance reform a signature issue, railed against Obama's hypocrisy for going back on his early campaign pledge to live within the federal limits. But voters didn't seem to care.

France's President Nicolas Sarkozy welcomes the candidate at the Élysée Palace in Paris. July 25, 2008.

Arriving for his speech in Berlin at the Victory Column. July 24, 2008.

Meanwhile, Hillary Clinton's supporters continued to press her vice-presidential claims. Obama had promised his supporters that he would announce his selection in a mass e-mail — which had the dividend of giving the campaign millions more contacts for getting out the vote in November. The pick was not Clinton but another one of the Democrats Obama had vanquished in the primaries, Senator Joseph R. Biden Jr. of Delaware. He was a safe choice who brought decades of experience in foreign affairs, helping to parry McCain's attacks that Obama was too light on national security.

Obama had promised his supporters that he would announce his selection in a mass e-mail.

The Democratic convention in Denver therefore featured the soap opera of whether the Clintons would fully embrace Obama, and Biden. Bill Clinton could still explode in rage over the way he and his wife had been portrayed during the primaries, especially the charge that they had played the race card. But at the convention, he gave a gracious endorsement that betrayed no lingering ill will. Hillary's speech, too, was warm and she rushed to the floor of the convention hall to make Obama's nomination unanimous on the eve of his acceptance speech.

Senator Obama's choice of Joseph Biden as his running mate was first announced via text message, then in person at a rally at the Old State Capitol in Springfield, Ill. August 23, 2008.

Guests lined up to have their pictures taken in front of a painting of Barack Obama at a party in Denver ahead of the Democratic National Convention. August 24, 2008.

"Many convention goers wandered around downtown still wearing their floor passes around their necks and hoisting printed 'Michelle' signs in the air. Others were plastered with bright blue face paint and Obama logos on hats, shirts and pants."

—From "Life of the Party: Roaming the Streets" by Julie Bosman on The Caucus Blog, nytimes.com, August 26, 2008

"**I**f one big task for Mr. Obama this week is to try to paint a critical picture of Mr. McCain and his policies, another is to try to present a fuller portrait of Mr. Obama and push back against Republicans' efforts to paint him as culturally and politically distant from mainstream America."

—*From "Appeals Evoking American Dream Rally Democrats" by Adam Nagourney, The New York Times, August 26, 2008*

Police on the perimeter of the convention at an anti-war protest. August 27, 2008.

PHOTOS: DAMON WINTER/NYT

"Last night Hillary told us in no uncertain terms that she is going to do everything she can to elect Barack Obama. That makes two of us."

—Bill Clinton, August 27, 2008

Former President Bill Clinton salutes the crowd after speaking at the Democratic Convention. August 27, 2008.

Senator Hillary Rodham Clinton at the podium on day two of the convention in Denver. August 26, 2008.

For the final night of the convention, the campaign had decided to move everyone, delegates and all, to Invesco Field at Mile High Stadium, where 80,000 people, some waiting in line for nearly a day, celebrated the new Democratic ticket.

The stage, draped with flags and lined with Greek columns, was meant to evoke the White House but some found the whole thing over the top.

"With profound gratitude and great humility, I accept your nomination for the presidency of the United States."

Obama took the stage on the 50-yard line to a blinding flicker of flashbulbs; toddlers waved small flags on their parents' shoulders; tears ran down elderly faces; and a roar befitting a Denver Broncos touchdown filled the stadium. "Change" signs formed a sea of blue, and chants of "USA!" competed with "Yes, we can!"

"With profound gratitude and great humility, I accept your nomination for the presidency of the United States," Obama began, the culmination of a marathon political carnival that bore little resemblance to any convention finale that had come before. The speech was being delivered on the 45th anniversary of Dr. Martin Luther King Jr.'s "I Have a Dream" speech, and Obama movingly referred to the throngs who had gathered at the Lincoln Memorial to hear "a young preacher from Georgia speak of his dream."

Surrounded by a capacity crowd, Barack Obama accepts his party's nomination and celebrates with the crowd and with his family. August 28, 2008.

THE AMERICAN PROMISE

AUGUST 28, 2008

To Chairman Dean and my great friend Dick Durbin; and to all my fellow citizens of this great nation; with profound gratitude and great humility, I accept your nomination for the presidency of the United States.

Let me express my thanks to the historic slate of candidates who accompanied me on this journey, and especially the one who traveled the farthest — a champion for working Americans and an inspiration to my daughters and to yours — Hillary Rodham Clinton. To President Clinton, who last night made the case for change as only he can make it; to Ted Kennedy, who embodies the spirit of service; and to the next vice president of the United States, Joe Biden, I thank you. I am grateful to finish this journey with one of the finest statesmen of our time, a man at ease with everyone from world leaders to the conductors on the Amtrak train he still takes home every night.

To the love of my life, our next first lady, Michelle Obama, and to Sasha and Malia — I love you so much, and I'm so proud of all of you.

TODD HEISLER/NYT

Four years ago, I stood before you and told you my story — of the brief union between a young man from Kenya and a young woman from Kansas who weren't well off or well known, but shared a belief that in America, their son could achieve whatever he put his mind to.

It is that promise that has always set this country apart — that through hard work and sacrifice, each of us can pursue our individual dreams but still come together as one American family, to ensure that the next generation can pursue their dreams as well.

That's why I stand here tonight. Because for 232 years, at each moment when that promise was in jeopardy, ordinary men and women — students and soldiers, farmers and teachers, nurses and janitors — found the courage to keep it alive.

We meet at one of those defining moments — a moment when our nation is at war, our economy is in turmoil, and the American promise has been threatened once more.

Tonight, more Americans are out of work and more are working harder for less. More of you have lost your homes and even more are watching your home values plummet. More of you have cars you can't afford to drive, credit card bills you can't afford to pay, and tuition that's beyond your reach.

These challenges are not all of government's making. But the failure to respond is a direct result of a broken politics in Washington and the failed policies of George W. Bush.

America, we are better than these last eight years. We are a better country than this.

This country is more decent than one where a woman in Ohio, on the brink of retirement, finds herself one illness away from disaster after a lifetime of hard work.

This country is more generous than one where a man in Indiana has to pack up the equipment he's worked on for 20 years and watch it shipped off to China, and then chokes up as he explains how he felt like a failure when he went home to tell his family the news.

We are more compassionate than a government that lets veterans sleep on our streets and families slide into poverty; that sits on its hands while a major American city drowns before our eyes.

Tonight, I say to the American people, to Democrats and Republicans and Independents across this great land — enough! This moment — this election — is our chance to keep, in the 21st century, the American promise alive. Because next week, in Minnesota, the same party that brought you two terms of George Bush and Dick Cheney will ask this country for a third. And we are here because we love this country too much to let the next four years look like the last eight. On November 4th, we must stand up and say: "Eight is enough."

Now let there be no doubt. The Republican nominee, John McCain, has worn the uniform of our country with bravery and distinction, and for that we owe him our gratitude and respect. And next week, we'll also hear about those occasions when he's broken with his party as evidence that he can deliver the change that we need.

But the record's clear: John McCain has voted with George Bush 90 percent of the time. Senator McCain likes to talk about judgment, but really, what does it say about your judgment when you think George Bush has been right more than 90 percent of the time? I don't know about you, but I'm not ready to take a 10 percent chance on change.

The truth is, on issue after issue that would make a difference in your lives — on health care and education and the economy — Senator McCain has been anything but independent. He said that our economy has made "great progress" under this president. He said that the fundamentals of the economy are strong. And when one of his chief advisers — the man who wrote his economic plan — was talking about the anxiety Americans are feeling, he said that we were just suffering from a "mental recession," and that we've become, and I quote, "a nation of whiners." A nation of whiners? Tell that to the proud auto workers at a Michigan plant who, after they found out it was closing, kept showing up every day and working as hard as ever, because they knew there were people who counted on the brakes that they made. Tell that to the military families who shoulder their burdens silently as they watch their loved ones leave for their third or fourth or fifth tour of duty. These are not whiners. They work hard and give back and keep going without complaint. These are the Americans that I know.

Now, I don't believe that Senator McCain doesn't care what's going on in the lives of Americans. I just think he doesn't know. Why else would he define middle class as someone making under five million dollars a year? How else could he propose hundreds of billions in tax breaks for big corporations and oil companies but not one penny of tax relief to more than 100 million Americans? How else could he offer a health care plan that would actually tax people's benefits, or an education plan that would do nothing to help families pay for college, or a plan that would privatize Social Security and gamble your retirement?

It's not because John McCain doesn't care. It's because John McCain doesn't get it.

For over two decades, he's subscribed to that old, discredited Republican philosophy — give more and more to those with the most and hope that prosperity trickles down to everyone else. In Washington, they call this the Ownership Society, but what it really means is — you're on your own. Out of work? Tough luck. No health care? The market will fix it. Born into poverty? Pull yourself up by your own bootstraps — even if you don't have boots. You're on your own.

Well it's time for them to own their failure. It's time for us to change America.

You see, we Democrats have a very different measure of what constitutes progress in this country.

We measure progress by how many people can find a job that pays the mortgage; whether you can put a little extra money away at the end of each month so you can someday watch your child receive her college diploma. We measure progress in the 23 million new jobs that were created when Bill Clinton was president — when the average American family saw its income go up $7,500 instead of down $2,000 like it has under George Bush.

We measure the strength of our economy not by the number of billionaires we have or the profits of the Fortune 500, but by whether someone with a good idea can take a risk and start a new business, or whether the waitress who lives on tips can take a day off to look after a sick kid without losing her job — an economy that honors the dignity of work.

The fundamentals we use to measure economic strength are whether we are living up to that fundamental promise that has made this country great — a promise that is the only reason I am standing here tonight.

Because in the faces of those young veterans who come back from Iraq and Afghanistan, I see my grandfather, who signed up after Pearl Harbor, marched in Patton's Army and was rewarded by a grateful nation with the chance to go to college on the G.I. Bill.

In the face of that young student who sleeps just three hours before working the night shift, I think about my mom, who raised my sister and me on her own while she worked and earned her degree; who once turned to food stamps but was still able to send us to the best schools in the country with the help of student loans and scholarships.

When I listen to another worker tell me that his factory has shut down, I remember all those men and women on the South Side of Chicago who I stood by and fought for two decades ago after the local steel plant closed.

And when I hear a woman talk about the difficulties of starting her own business, I think about my grandmother, who worked her way up from the secretarial pool to middle-man-

That's the promise of America — the idea that we are responsible for ourselves, but that we also rise or fall as one nation.

agement, despite years of being passed over for promotions because she was a woman. She's the one who taught me about hard work. She's the one who put off buying a new car or a new dress for herself so that I could have a better life. She poured everything she had into me. And although she can no longer travel, I know that she's watching tonight, and that tonight is her night as well.

I don't know what kind of lives John McCain thinks that celebrities lead, but this has been mine. These are my heroes. Theirs are the stories that shaped me. And it is on their behalf that I intend to win this election and keep our promise alive as president of the United States.

What is that promise?

It's a promise that says each of us has the freedom to make of our own lives what we will, but that we also have the obligation to treat each other with dignity and respect.

It's a promise that says the market should reward drive and innovation and generate growth, but that businesses should live up to

THE AMERICAN PROMISE
AUGUST 28, 2008

their responsibilities to create American jobs, look out for American workers, and play by the rules of the road.

Ours is a promise that says government cannot solve all our problems, but what it should do is that which we cannot do for ourselves — protect us from harm and provide every child a decent education; keep our water clean and our toys safe; invest in new schools and new roads and new science and technology.

Our government should work for us, not against us. It should help us, not hurt us. It should ensure opportunity not just for those with the most money and influence, but for every American who's willing to work.

That's the promise of America — the idea that we are responsible for ourselves, but that we also rise or fall as one nation; the fundamental belief that I am my brother's keeper; I am my sister's keeper.

That's the promise we need to keep. That's the change we need right now. So let me spell out exactly what that change would mean if I am president.

Change means a tax code that doesn't reward the lobbyists who wrote it, but the American workers and small businesses who deserve it.

Unlike John McCain, I will stop giving tax breaks to corporations that ship jobs overseas, and I will start giving them to companies that create good jobs right here in America.

I will eliminate capital gains taxes for the small businesses and the start-ups that will create the high-wage, high-tech jobs of tomorrow.

I will cut taxes — cut taxes — for 95 percent of all working families. Because in an economy like this, the last thing we should do is raise taxes on the middle class.

And for the sake of our economy, our security and the future of our planet, I will set a clear goal as president: in 10 years, we will finally end our dependence on oil from the Middle East.

Washington's been talking about our oil addiction for the last 30 years, and John McCain has been there for 26 of them. In that time, he's said no to higher fuel-efficiency standards for cars, no to investments in renewable energy, no to renewable fuels. And today, we import triple the amount of oil as the day that Senator McCain took office.

Now is the time to end this addiction, and to understand that drilling is a stop-gap measure, not a long-term solution. Not even close.

As president, I will tap our natural-gas reserves, invest in clean-coal technology and find ways to safely harness nuclear power. I'll help our auto companies re-tool, so that the fuel-efficient cars of the future are built right here in America. I'll make it easier for the American

people to afford these new cars. And I'll invest 150 billion dollars over the next decade in affordable, renewable sources of energy — wind power and solar power and the next generation of biofuels; an investment that will lead to new industries and five million new jobs that pay well and can't ever be outsourced.

America, now is not the time for small plans.

Now is the time to finally meet our moral obligation to provide every child a world-class education, because it will take nothing less to compete in the global economy. Michelle and I are only here tonight because we were given a chance at an education. And I will not settle for an America where some kids don't have that chance. I'll invest in early childhood education. I'll recruit an army of new teachers, and pay them higher salaries and give them more support. And in exchange, I'll ask for higher standards and more accountability. And we will keep our promise to every young American — if you commit to serving your community or your country, we will make sure you can afford a college education.

Now is the time to finally keep the promise of affordable, accessible health care for every single American. If you have health care, my plan will lower your premiums. If you don't, you'll be able to get the same kind of coverage that members of Congress give themselves. And as someone who watched my mother argue with insurance companies while she lay in bed dying of cancer, I will make certain those companies stop discriminating against those who are sick and need care the most.

Now is the time to help families with paid sick days and better family leave, because nobody in America should have to choose between keeping their jobs and caring for a sick child or ailing parent.

Now is the time to change our bankruptcy laws, so that your pensions are protected ahead of CEO bonuses; and the time to protect Social Security for future generations.

And now is the time to keep the promise of equal pay for an equal day's work, because I want my daughters to have exactly the same opportunities as your sons.

Now, many of these plans will cost money, which is why I've laid out how I'll pay for every dime — by closing corporate loopholes and tax havens that don't help America grow. But I will also go through the federal budget, line by line, eliminating programs that no longer work and making the ones we do need work better and cost less — because we cannot meet 21st-century challenges with a 20th-century bureaucracy.

And Democrats, we must also admit that fulfilling America's promise will require more than just money. It will require a renewed

We need a President who can face the threats of the future, not keep grasping at the ideas of the past.

sense of responsibility from each of us to recover what John F. Kennedy called our "intellectual and moral strength." Yes, government must lead on energy independence, but each of us must do our part to make our homes and businesses more efficient. Yes, we must provide more ladders to success for young men who fall into lives of crime and despair. But we must also admit that programs alone can't replace parents; that government can't turn off the television and make a child do her homework; that fathers must take more responsibility for providing the love and guidance their children need.

Individual responsibility and mutual responsibility — that's the essence of America's promise.

And just as we keep our promise to the next generation here at home, so must we keep America's promise abroad. If John McCain wants to have a debate about who has the temperament, and judgment, to serve as the next commander in chief, that's a debate I'm ready to have.

For while Senator McCain was turning his sights to Iraq just days after 9/11, I stood up and opposed this war, knowing that it would distract us from the real threats we face. When John McCain said we could just "muddle through" in Afghanistan, I argued for more resources and more troops to finish the fight against the terrorists who actually attacked us on 9/11, and made clear that we must take out Osama bin Laden and his lieutenants if we have them in our sights. John McCain likes to say that he'll follow bin Laden to the gates of hell — but he won't even go to the cave where he lives.

And today, as my call for a time frame to remove our troops from Iraq has been echoed by the Iraqi government and even the Bush administration, even after we learned that Iraq has a $79 billion surplus while we're wallowing in deficits, John McCain stands alone in his stubborn refusal to end a misguided war.

That's not the judgment we need. That won't keep America safe. We need a president who can face the threats of the future, not keep grasping at the ideas of the past.

You don't defeat a terrorist network that operates in 80 countries by occupying Iraq. You don't protect Israel and deter Iran just by talking tough in Washington. You can't truly stand up for Georgia when you've strained our oldest alliances. If John McCain wants to follow George Bush with more tough talk and bad strategy, that is his choice — but it is not the change we need.

We are the party of Roosevelt. We are the party of Kennedy. So don't tell me that Democrats won't defend this country. Don't tell me that Democrats won't keep us safe. The Bush-McCain foreign policy

has squandered the legacy that generations of Americans — Democrats and Republicans — have built, and we are here to restore that legacy.

As commander in chief, I will never hesitate to defend this nation, but I will only send our troops into harm's way with a clear mission and a sacred commitment to give them the equipment they need in battle and the care and benefits they deserve when they come home.

I will end this war in Iraq responsibly, and finish the fight against al Qaeda and the Taliban in Afghanistan. I will rebuild our military to meet future conflicts. But I will also renew the tough, direct diplomacy that can prevent Iran from obtaining nuclear weapons and curb Russian aggression. I will build new partnerships to defeat the threats of the 21st century: terrorism and nuclear proliferation; poverty and genocide; climate change and disease. And I will restore our moral standing, so that America is once again that last, best hope for all who are called to the cause of freedom, who long for lives of peace and who yearn for a better future.

These are the policies I will pursue. And in the weeks ahead, I look forward to debating them with John McCain.

But what I will not do is suggest that the Senator takes his positions for political purposes. Because one of the things that we have to change in our politics is the idea that people cannot disagree without challenging each other's character and patriotism.

What nay-sayers don't understand is that this election has never been about me. It's been about you.

The times are too serious, the stakes are too high for this same partisan playbook. So let us agree that patriotism has no party. I love this country, and so do you, and so does John McCain. The men and women who serve in our battlefields may be Democrats and Republicans and Independents, but they have fought together and bled together and some died together under the same proud flag. They have not served a red America or a blue America — they have served the United States of America.

So I've got news for you, John McCain. We all put our country first.

America, our work will not be easy. The challenges we face require tough choices, and Democrats as well as Republicans will need to cast off the worn-out ideas and politics of the past. For part of what has been lost these past eight years can't just be measured by lost wages or bigger trade deficits. What has also been lost is our sense of common purpose — our sense of higher purpose. And that's what we have to restore.

We may not agree on abortion, but surely we can agree on reducing the number of unwanted pregnancies in this country. The reality of gun ownership may be different for hunters in rural Ohio than for those plagued by gang violence in Cleveland, but don't tell me we

THE AMERICAN PROMISE
AUGUST 28, 2008

can't uphold the Second Amendment while keeping AK-47s out of the hands of criminals. I know there are differences on same-sex marriage, but surely we can agree that our gay and lesbian brothers and sisters deserve to visit the person they love in the hospital and to live lives free of discrimination. Passions fly on immigration, but I don't know anyone who benefits when a mother is separated from her infant child or an employer undercuts American wages by hiring illegal workers. This too is part of America's promise — the promise of a democracy where we can find the strength and grace to bridge divides and unite in common effort.

I know there are those who dismiss such beliefs as happy talk. They claim that our insistence on something larger, something firmer and more honest in our public life is just a Trojan Horse for higher taxes and the abandonment of traditional values. And that's to be expected. Because if you don't have any fresh ideas, then you use stale tactics to scare the voters. If you don't have a record to run on, then you paint your opponent as someone people should run from.

You make a big election about small things.

And you know what — it's worked before. Because it feeds into the cynicism we all have about government. When Washington doesn't work, all its promises seem empty. If your hopes have been dashed again and again, then it's best to stop hoping, and settle for what you already know.

I get it. I realize that I am not the likeliest candidate for this office. I don't fit the typical pedigree, and I haven't spent my career in the halls of Washington.

But I stand before you tonight because all across America something is stirring. What the naysayers don't understand is that this election has never been about me. It's been about you.

For 18 long months, you have stood up, one by one, and said "enough" to the politics of the past. You understand that in this election, the greatest risk we can take is to try the same old politics with the same old players and expect a different result. You have shown what history teaches us — that at defining moments like this one, the change we need doesn't come from Washington. Change comes to Washington. Change happens because the American people demand it — because they rise up and insist on new ideas and new leadership, a new politics for a new time.

America, this is one of those moments.

I believe that as hard as it will be, the change we need is coming. Because I've seen it. Because I've lived it. I've seen it in Illinois, when we provided health care to more children and moved more families from welfare to work. I've seen it in Washington, when we worked across party lines to open up government and hold lobbyists more accountable, to give better care for our veterans and keep nuclear weapons out of terrorist hands.

And I've seen it in this campaign. In the young people who voted for the first time, and in those who got involved again after a very long time. In the Republicans who never thought they'd pick up a Democratic ballot, but did. I've seen it in the workers who would rather cut their hours back a day than see their friends lose their jobs, in the soldiers who re-enlist after losing a limb, in the good neighbors who take a stranger in when a hurricane strikes and the floodwaters rise.

This country of ours has more wealth than any nation, but that's not what makes us rich. We have the most powerful military on Earth, but that's not what makes us strong. Our universities and our culture are the envy of the world, but that's not what keeps the world coming to our shores.

America, we cannot turn back. We cannot walk alone.

Instead, it is that American spirit — that American promise — that pushes us forward even when the path is uncertain; that binds us together in spite of our differences; that makes us fix our eye not on what is seen, but what is unseen, that better place around the bend.

That promise is our greatest inheritance. It's a promise I make to my daughters when I tuck them in at night, and a promise that you make to yours — a promise that has led immigrants to cross oceans and pioneers to travel west; a promise that led workers to picket lines, and women to reach for the ballot.

And it is that promise that 45 years ago today brought Americans from every corner of this land to stand together on a mall in Washington, before the Lincoln Memorial, and hear a young preacher from Georgia speak of his dream.

The men and women who gathered there could've heard many things. They could've heard words of anger and discord. They could've been told to succumb to the fear and frustration of so many dreams deferred.

But what the people heard instead — people of every creed and color, from every walk of life — is that in America, our destiny is inextricably linked. That together, our dreams can be one.

"We cannot walk alone," the preacher cried. "And as we walk, we must make the pledge that we shall always march ahead. We cannot turn back."

America, we cannot turn back. Not with so much work to be done. Not with so many children to educate, and so many veterans to care for. Not with an economy to fix and cities to rebuild and farms to save. Not with so many families to protect and so many lives to mend. America, we cannot turn back. We cannot walk alone. At this moment, in this election, we must pledge once more to march into the future. Let us keep that promise — that American promise — and in the words of Scripture hold firmly, without wavering, to the hope that we confess.

Thank you, God bless you, and God bless the United States of America. ◆

Barack and Michelle Obama celebrate his nomination in Denver, Colo.
August 28, 2008.

Despite the euphoria in Denver, John McCain appeared to gain ground after the Republican convention in St. Paul, Minn. McCain's choice of a young female governor, Sarah Palin of Alaska, energized the party's conservative base. Others, though, deemed the choice a disaster because it undermined McCain's major campaign theme, experience.

Palin had been in office only a few years and before becoming Alaska's governor she was the mayor of a tiny town, Wasilla, and was a self-described Hockey Mom. After rejoicing over her strong convention acceptance speech, in which she relentlessly attacked and mocked Obama, the McCain campaign kept her closeted from the national media. Then, after overcoaching her, they scheduled interviews with the network anchors. Palin's performance during an interview with Katie Couric, in which she stumbled repeatedly over relatively simple questions and spoke in almost comic non sequiturs, went viral on YouTube and became fodder for a barrage of brutally comic skits on "Saturday Night Live." A $150,000-plus spending spree on clothes financed by the Republican National Committee tarnished her image even more.

> ## McCain's choice of a young female governor, Sarah Palin of Alaska, energized the party's conservative base.

Once the campaign turned to party against party, the dynamics changed. Unlike in the primaries, where Obama and Clinton had agreed on more issues than not, Obama and McCain had extremely divergent worldviews.

Their most profound differences were over the war in Iraq. McCain still spoke of "victory" and opposed setting dates for extracting American troops. Obama was an early opponent of the war, and he presented a military and diplomatic plan for withdrawing American forces. He also warned that until the Pentagon began pulling troops out of Iraq, there would not be enough troops to defeat the Taliban and Al Qaeda in Afghanistan. He blamed President Bush for taking his focus off defeating Al Qaeda and becoming distracted by Iraq.

They differed over government's proper role in people's lives. McCain was an economic conservative who railed against wasteful government spending and appropriations called earmarks.

Republican presidential candidate John McCain and his running mate, Alaska Governor Sarah Palin, at a rally in Washington, Pa. August 30, 2008.

STEPHEN CROWLEY/NYT

Ghosts from Chicago

In addition to his relationship with Rev. Wright, Barack Obama's ties to two other men he met in Chicago would be questioned by his political foes.

With two best-selling books and national celebrity gained from his convention keynote, in 2005 the Obamas had real money for the first time in their lives. They set their sights on a red-brick, Georgian Revival mansion with white columns in the Kenwood District of Chicago's Hyde Park, purchased for around $1.65 million. Besides the house, they purchased a strip of vacant land next door from a lot that had been bought at the same time by a wheeler-dealer named Antoin (Tony) Rezko, who was an Obama friend and supporter.

Rezko, 52, owned a lot of property in Chicago and Barack Obama had encountered him during his organizing days. Because of his high profile in housing and political clout, Rezko was well known throughout the city and had raised about $150,000 for Obama's campaigns at the state level. But after Rezko was indicted on fraud charges, Obama returned the donations.

The Obamas had purchased a strip of the lot from Rezko's wife to expand their yard, but after Rezko faced mounting business problems and, later, corruption charges, questions arose over the deal. Although the Obama campaign spent hours with a team from the Chicago Tribune poring over the real estate transaction in an attempt to prove that he had not received preferred, below-market terms, the stain remained.

Still, no evidence surfaced in the courtroom to suggest that Obama was involved in any wrongdoing. In June 2008 a federal jury found Rezko guilty of 16 counts, including fraud, money laundering and bribery, in an influence-peddling scheme that touched the highest levels of the administration of Gov. Rod R. Blagojevich of Illinois.

Bill Ayers was yet another character from Obama's Chicago past who found himself with a walk-on part in the national political drama.

At a tumultuous meeting of anti-Vietnam War militants at the Chicago Coliseum in 1969, Ayers helped found the radical Weathermen, launching a campaign of bombings that would target the Pentagon and the United States Capitol.

Twenty-six years later, at a lunchtime meeting in a Chicago skyscraper about school reform, Barack Obama met Ayers, by then

Rezko in May 2008.

JOHN GRESS/REUTERS

Ayers in 1980.

CHARLES KNOBLOCK/AP

an education professor at the University of Illinois at Chicago. Their paths have crossed sporadically since then, at a coffee Ayers hosted for Obama's first run for office, on the schools project and a charitable board and in casual encounters as Hyde Park neighbors.

But during the presidential campaign, their relationship became a touchstone for Obama opponents. The issue was first raised by the Clinton campaign, but the McCain-Palin ticket made Ayers a centerpiece of their attacks, with Sarah Palin accusing Obama of "palling around with terrorists." Video clips on You-Tube juxtaposed Obama's face with the young Ayers or grainy shots of the bombings.

A New York Times review of records of the schools project and interviews with a dozen people who know both men suggested that Obama played down his contacts with Ayers, 64. But the two men were never close and Obama never expressed sympathy for the radical views and actions of Ayers, whom he has called "somebody who engaged in detestable acts 40 years ago, when I was 8."

The men first met in 1995 through the education project, the Chicago Annenberg Challenge, and encountered each other occasionally in public life or around Hyde Park. They last met more than a year ago when they bumped into each other on the street in Hyde Park.

The education project that brought them together was part of a national school reform effort financed with $500 million from Walter H. Annenberg, the billionaire publisher and philanthropist and President Richard M. Nixon's ambassador to the United Kingdom. Many cities applied for the Annenberg money, and Ayers joined two other local education activists to lead a broad, citywide effort that won nearly $50 million for Chicago.

In March 1995, Obama became chairman of the six-member board that oversaw the distribution of grants in Chicago. Ayers had nothing to do with Obama's appointment.

After the election, interest in Ayers died down. He promoted a new edition of his 2001 memoir and wrote an Op-Ed piece for The New York Times, "The Real Bill Ayers." He said he had been unfairly demonized in the campaign and was not close to Obama. "I knew him as well as thousands of others did," he wrote, "and like millions of others, I wish I knew him better."

The Scars of Yesterday

Obama and Lewis, Selma, Ala.
March 4, 2007.

The veterans of the March on Washington were the living connective tissue to the America of 1963, when the police in some cities and towns still beat blacks with truncheons, and the story of their journey was as complicated as race itself.

At least five veterans of that March traveled to Denver as Democratic delegates in August 2008, among them Representative John Lewis of Georgia, who is the last man alive of the 10 who spoke that April day at the Lincoln Memorial. This son of sharecroppers, who was almost beaten to death by police officers in Selma, Ala., when he marched with civil rights activists across a bridge, stood on a sun-splashed street in Denver and considered the distance traveled.

His bald head still bears nearly half-century-old scars.

"We've had disappointments since then, but if someone told me I would be here," Lewis said, shaking that head. "When people say nothing has changed, I feel like saying, 'Come walk in my shoes.'"

Barack Obama was still a toddler when John Lewis was on the barricades of the civil rights movement. Still, for those sharing a generation with the Rev. Dr. Martin Luther King Jr., Obama's nomination had a singular resonance.

Dezie Woods-Jones was with the California delegation at the convention. Now in her 60s, she had also been in Washington to hear Dr. King speak about his dream.

"I was young, naïve enough to think I would see that in five, ten years," she said. "Then you see leaders killed, you see police brutality, residential segregation in cities. About 10 years ago I thought: I won't see this. This is something for my grandchildren."

She paused, her eyes now red-rimmed.

"What to say except, 'Oh, hallelujah!'" she said. "We have a lot of work, a lot, but we are so much closer than I expected."

A Quiet Voice Speaks Out

Former Secretary of State Colin L. Powell had dealt with prejudice in his life, in and out of the Army, and as a kid of Jamaican heritage growing up in Harlem and the South Bronx.

Powell, who had served three Republican presidents, went on NBC's "Meet the Press" in October and told Tom Brokaw that he was troubled by what other Republicans, though not John McCain, had said: "'Well, you know that Mr. Obama is a Muslim.' Well, the correct answer is, he is not a Muslim. He's a Christian. He's always been a Christian. But the really right answer is, what if he is? Is there something wrong with being a Muslim in this country? The answer's no. That's not America. Is something wrong with some 7-year-old Muslim-American kid believing that he or she could be president?"

Breaking with his party to endorse Barack Obama was, for a military man trained in loyalty, a bold move, one intended to help both the candidate and himself. It was not only an embrace of a presidential candidate from the other party, but also an effort to reshape a legacy that he himself considered tainted by his service under President George W. Bush.

The endorsement, which came after months of conversations between Powell and Obama on a wide range of foreign and domestic policy issues, made clear Powell's dismay at the Republican Party. He said he felt that the party had become too conservative under Bush, and that McCain's campaign was not good for the country or its reputation around the world.

Powell himself had thought about running for president 13 years earlier. Instead, he had joined the Bush administration and helped sell the Iraq war before the United Nations. His reputation had suffered, but the reaction to the Obama endorsement seemed to restore some of its luster.

"God bless General Powell for saying openly what I had always understood to be the credo of this country — freedom for all, irrespective of nationality, race or religion," wrote Times reader Keith B. Braun.

Gen. Colin Powell on "Meet the Press." October 19, 2008.

"Senator John McCain astonished the political world on Friday by naming Sarah Palin, a little-known governor of Alaska and self-described 'hockey mom' with almost no foreign policy experience, as his running mate on the Republican presidential ticket."

—*From "Alaskan Is McCain's Choice; First Woman on G.O.P. Ticket" by Michael Cooper and Elisabeth Bumiller, The New York Times, August 29, 2008*

Senators Obama and Biden with voters in Hamilton, Ind. August 31, 2008.

OZIER MUHAMMAD/NYT

In his convention speech in Denver, Obama said: "Government cannot solve all our problems, but what it should do is that which we cannot do for ourselves: protect us from harm and provide every child a decent education; keep our water clean and our toys safe; invest in new schools and new roads and new science and technology." He favored raising the minimum wage and tying it to inflation.

Both candidates denounced torture and were committed to closing the prison camp in Guantánamo Bay, Cuba. But Obama went further and promised to identify and correct the Bush administration's abuse of executive power. McCain promised improved protections for detainees, but he had helped the White House push through the Military Commissions Act of 2006, which denied detainees the right to a court hearing and put Washington in conflict with the Geneva Conventions.

"The fundamentals of our economy are strong," [McCain] said, words that some believed doomed his candidacy.

They differed sharply on the kinds of justices they would appoint to the Supreme Court. Obama favored abortion rights, McCain opposed them and promised to continue the court's tilt to the right.

In this campaign, McCain abandoned his prior, moderate positions on climate change and immigration reform. Earlier in his career, McCain had offered the first plausible bill to control America's emissions of greenhouse gases. But his positions had changed, though not quite to the extent that he embraced the simple energy plan of Palin, who led chants of: "drill, baby, drill."

Obama presented himself as an environmental protector who would strictly control the emissions of greenhouse gases. He endorsed some offshore drilling, but as part of a comprehensive strategy including big investments in new, clean technologies. He promised to create thousands of new "green collar" jobs.

Right before the candidates' first debate, the economy cratered. Lehman Brothers collapsed, a harrowing indicator of the coming financial crisis and a reminder that the presidential

The candidate consults his advisers after a foreign policy meeting in Richmond, Va. October 22, 2008.

Presidential candidates Barack Obama and John McCain in the third and final presidential debate at Hofstra University in Hempstead, N.Y. October 15, 2008.

LIVE FROM NEW YORK!

With her signature black glasses, Sarah Palin bore an uncanny resemblance to Tina Fey, the creator of NBC's "30 Rock," and former "Saturday Night Live" writer and star. Soon Fey was back on "SNL" doing an impersonation of Palin so deliciously dead-on that it helped the show score its highest ratings in years. The popularity of those Palin parodies (at times, Fey quoted the Alaska governor verbatim) began to overshadow the real vice-presidential nominee.

Fey, along with another "SNL" star, Amy Poehler, who played the CBS anchor Katie Couric (in a previous skit, Poehler had played Hillary Rodham Clinton), parodied Palin's performance during the interview. When it came to a question about spreading democracy abroad, Fey, relying on game-show terminology, said, "Katie, I'd like to use one of my lifelines," adding later, "I want to phone a friend."

Tina Fey as Gov. Sarah Palin in a "Saturday Night Live" skit. September 13, 2008.

DANA EDELSON/NBC

There was one real-life debate between the vice-presidential candidates and most analysts considered it a wash. Palin, stressing her likeability, gamely walked up to Biden and asked, "Can I call you Joe?"

Alessandra Stanley of The Times wrote that in the debate, "Sarah Palin got the better of Sarah Palin. The debate wasn't so much between Senator Joseph R. Biden Jr. and Ms. Palin as it was between the dueling images of the Alaska governor: the fuzzy-minded amateur parodied — with her own words — by Tina Fey on 'Saturday Night Live' or the gun-toting hockey mom who blazed into history at the Republican convention.

"There was a little of both on stage Thursday night."

Fey made her final appearance as Palin on "SNL" alongside the real John McCain. They appeared with Cindy McCain, in a skit where the money-strapped McCain-Palin ticket went on the QVC shopping network to "sell stuff" to raise funds for the campaign.

campaign was turning into a referendum on which candidate could best address the nation's economic challenges.

Speaking at an almost empty convention center in Jacksonville, Fla., on Sept. 15, McCain was trying to show concern for the prospect of hardship but also optimism about the country's resilience.

"The fundamentals of our economy are strong," he said, words that some believed doomed his candidacy.

A thousand miles away, at Obama headquarters in Chicago, his aides knew immediately that they had just heard a potential turning point in a race that seemed to be tightening. They rushed out to tell Dan Pfeiffer, the Obama communications director, what McCain had just said, knowing that it could be used to portray their opponent as out of touch.

The McCain campaign team often seemed to make missteps and lurch from moment to moment in search of a consistent strategy.

"Shut up!" Pfeiffer said incredulously. "He said what?" Obama, who had just arrived at a rally in Colorado, hastily inserted the comments into his speech. By nightfall, the Obama campaign had produced an advertisement that included video of McCain making the statement, a vision that would shadow him for the rest of the campaign.

At the McCain campaign headquarters in Arlington, Va., at almost the same moment that morning, McCain's chief strategist, Steve Schmidt, looked stricken when his war room alerted him to the comment. Within 30 minutes, he was headed for a flight to Florida to join McCain as they began a frantic and ultimately unsuccessful effort to recover.

McCain's inartful phrase, and the responses of the two campaigns, fundamentally altered the dynamic of the race. But the episode also highlighted a deeper difference: the McCain campaign team often seemed to make missteps and lurch from moment to moment in search of a consistent strategy and message, while the disciplined and nimble Obama team marched through a presidential contest of historic intensity learning to exploit opponents' weaknesses and making remarkably few stumbles.

DOUG MILLS/NYT

With the view of his teleprompter, Obama pauses while speaking at a rally in Springfield, Mo. November 1, 2008.

on his cell phone aboard his campaign plane, Springfield, Mo.

"I hope you guys are up for a fight. I hope you guys are game because I haven't been putting up with 19 months of airplanes and hotel food and missing my babies and my wife — I didn't put up with that stuff just to come in second."

—From "Obama: 'I Don't Believe in Coming in Second'" by Jeff Zeleny on The Caucus Blog, nytimes.com, September 6, 2008

On the tarmac in Chicago after a trip to Fayetteville, N.C. October 19, 2008

Senator Obama meets Joe Wurzelbacher, aka Joe the Plumber, in Holland, Ohio. Joe soon became a household name, thanks to Senator McCain invoking him frequently in a presidential debate. October 12, 2008.

From there, McCain staggered forward. He announced he was suspending his campaign to return to Washington to help solve the financial crisis, suggesting he might skip the first debate. When he arrived in Washington, Republicans balked at approving the bailout plan and McCain could not mediate the impasse. So the debate was suddenly back on.

After this wild ride, Obama's calm performance in their first debate made him appear presidential. While McCain jabbed at him during the debate, he did not look at Obama once in 90 minutes, despite rules that encouraged them to speak directly to each other.

> *As the race wore on, some of the final McCain and Palin rallies turned ugly. Someone in the crowd yelled "Treason!" when Obama's name was mentioned.*

The second and third debates were really no better. McCain tediously repeated the phrase "My friends," as the overture to his answers and, in the third, he endlessly invoked Joe the Plumber, a middle-class Everyman who McCain insisted would see his taxes balloon under Obama's economic plan. In various polls, Obama was deemed the winner of all three debates. Well-prepared and commanding, if not exciting, he came across as a plausible president.

As the race wore on, some of the final McCain and Palin rallies turned ugly. Someone in the crowd yelled "Treason!" when Obama's name was mentioned. In Lakeville, Minn., a woman took the microphone and told McCain, "I can't trust Obama. I have read about him, and he's not, he's not, he's a, hum, he's an Arab."

McCain had had enough and his sense of honor took hold. "No, ma'am," the senator responded firmly. "He's not. He's a decent family man, a citizen, that I just happen to have disagreements with on fundamental issues; that's what this campaign is about. He's not. Thank you."

Signing books at Mountain Range High School in Westminster, Colo. September 29, 2008.

The candidate runs to the stage during a rally at Knology Park, Dunedin, Fla. September 24, 2008.

A rally in Jacksonville, Fla. September 20, 2008.

DAMON WINTER/NYT

*Speaking at a rally under the watchful eye of law enforcement agents, Pueblo, Colo.
November 1, 2008.*

The negative tone of the campaign and the murmurings about Obama being a Muslim had a powerful impact on one disgusted Republican, former Secretary of State Colin L. Powell. During an appearance on "Meet the Press" in late October, Powell broke with his party and endorsed Obama.

The audience for Obama's program far exceeded the expectations of television executives, and quieted many political pundits who questioned whether Obama was engaging in overkill.

With plenty of money still flowing into the campaign during the final month, Obama bought a half-hour of national television time for a glossy infomercial. A smashing ratings success, the commercial proved to be more popular than even the final game of the World Series — or last season's finale of "American Idol." The audience for Obama's program far exceeded the expectations of television executives, and quieted many political pundits who questioned whether Obama was engaging in overkill in buying a half hour on so many networks.

The commercial played on seven networks, broadcast and cable, and was seen by 33.55 million viewers, according to figures released by Nielsen Media Research. On the three broadcast networks that carried the special, the audience totaled more than 25 million. "I was shocked by the number Obama was able to draw," said Leslie Moonves, the chairman of CBS. "It's just a stunning number."

Now, it seemed, all the campaign had to worry about was overconfidence. And that was not likely to happen, either among Obama's closest advisers, his thousands of volunteers or the millions of supporters who had waited four years — or more realistically, eight — for the opportunity to make things different. True, the polls were leaning in their man's direction, but nothing was going to be taken for granted. And as Nov. 4 drew nearer, a palpable tension was in the air. Many people could not remember a more important day. ♦

The jacket comes off at a rainy rally in Fredericksburg, Va. September 27, 2008.

DOUG MILLS/NYT

Arrows on the floor of the stage indicate Sen. Obama's exit route, Austin, Tex. February 28, 2008.

Trying to get a smile out of a baby, Bozeman, Mont. May 19, 2008.

The Obamas unite on stage in Springfield, Mo. November 1, 2008.

Waiting backstage at Richmond Coliseum in Richmond, Va. October 22, 2008.

"He has the gift of making people see themselves in him and offers an enigmatic smile when asked about his multiracial appeal. 'I am like a Rorschach test,' he said in an interview with The New York Times. 'Even if people find me disappointing ultimately, they might gain something.'"

—From "Barack Obama: Calm in the Swirl of History" by Michael Powell, The New York Times, June 4, 2008

Senator Obama reaching out to supporters in Harrisonburg, Va. October 28, 2008.

Ahead in the polls as the election nears, Obama speaks in Springfield, Mo. November 1, 2008.

The bleachers at a campaign rally at Bonanza High School in Las Vegas, Nev. October 25, 2008.

THE ART OF POLITICS

ROB WALKER

Whether or not Barack Obama would make a good president, it's clear that he makes an excellent muse. It's hard to think of a political candidate in recent memory who has, in real time, inspired so much creativity, exercised free of charge and for the campaign's benefit. Perhaps this suggests something about Obama — or maybe it suggests something about his supporters.

The examples are many. One of the most prominent is the limited-edition print created by the Los Angeles artist Shepard Fairey in January. Fairey is best known as the creator of the "Obey Giant" imagery that, beginning in 1989, spread on city streets around the world by way of posters, stickers and stencils. (Disclosure: I contributed an essay to Fairey's 2006 book, "Obey: Supply & Demand," an extensive survey of that project and of his career so far.) Fairey made a brief statement when he unveiled the portrait, noting his "great conviction that Barack Obama should be the next President." Poster sales, he added, would underwrite "a large statewide poster campaign."

In addition to popping up on many streets, the image later made its way onto a T-shirt, created in collaboration with the San Francisco street-wear brand Upper Playground — and apparently onto the radar of the Obama campaign. The candidate himself sent a thank-you note, and his campaign had Fairey create a new poster that became the inaugural offering in an "Artists for Obama" section of the barackobama online store. Fairey told Creativity Online that while he has been politically active, there's something new in the enthusiasm he now professes to feel. "I just thought it was time to stick my neck out," he said. A variety of other artists apparently feel something similar. A California art duo known as the Date Farmers created an Obama screen print in an edition of 300; add the pro-Obama prints by Sam Flores, MAC and Munk One, and you're on your way to a hipster gallery show.

Meanwhile, will.i.am of the Black Eyed Peas created a video that remixed an Obama speech into a song, with a variety of music-celebrity contributors joining in on the candidate's oft-cited slogan, "Yes, we can." It's had more than 6.5 million YouTube views and inspired spinoffs, including a "No, you can't" video by the satirical Billionaires for Bush. As Advertising Age has noted, a variety of ad-world "creatives" (it's actually a job title in that industry) have also cooked up freelance online videos and the like, free. The grass-roots end of the creativity spectrum has included ObamaOfDreams.com, which offered T-shirts on which baseball team logos were tweaked to read "Obama" (until Major League Baseball intervened), and a D.I.Y. "O'bama" St. Patrick's Day dress recently featured on Craftzine.com.

Creative types have backed politicians before, and Obama does not have a monopoly on such expression even in the Democratic primary. (There's Jack Nicholson's somewhat strange pro-Clinton clip made up of spliced-together movie performances, for instance.) But the Obama endorsements seem not simply expressions of support, but of something more like fandom. Dan Ariely, a behavioral-economics professor at M.I.T. and author of the recent book "Predictably Irrational," has gone so far as to compare it to romance, citing research about the early stages of dating as a comparison point: "When we get partial information about others we tend to fill in the gaps optimistically; we assume that they are wonderful, just like us and that they share our exact values and preferences." He figures part of Obama's charm may be the way fans are filling in the blanks.

This brings us to perhaps the most delightful piece of Obama-inspired creativity, the Web site barackobamaisyournewbicycle.com. This is nothing but a series of statements about the wonderful things Obama has done for "you." He left a comment on your blog, picked you up at the airport, built you a robot, thinks you are cute and, sweetly: "Barack Obama has a balloon for you." The site has been read as support — and as a satire of crush-blind Obama supporters. Of course this ambiguity is what makes it so pleasing. Because perfect little things like this are invariably converted into profitable objects, a deal has been struck to release an illustrated book based on the site. The stated goal to get it into stores before the Democratic convention reflects a reality lurking behind the political optimism: all the creative expression in the world doesn't guarantee that we'll ever find out what sort of president Obama might be.

The New York Times Magazine, April 13, 2008

Iconography inspired by Barack Obama.

America, It's Up to Us

BOB HERBERT

Barack Obama didn't just win the White House; he raised hopes and expectations around the world. Hyperbole burst like a rocket through its already excessive limits and went streaking to new heights.

"How to Fix the World," said a cover headline on Newsweek magazine, next to a large photo of the president-elect stepping jauntily onto a plane deliberately meant to mimic Air Force One.

Another magazine showed Obama and two of his sidekicks in Superman costumes, with the president-elect — his right fist raised and his red cape rippling behind him — having just achieved liftoff. The headline said simply: "Saving the World."

It would take a superman to haul the United States (forget the rest of the world for a moment) out of the sinkhole of troubles that Obama inherited. The economy had fallen into its worst downturn since the Depression. Banks were going under. Wall Street giants like Bear Stearns and Merrill Lynch found it impossible to survive in their original incarnations, and mighty Lehman Brothers was unable to survive at all.

The automobile industry, the backbone of American manufacturing and the fountainhead of the middle class, was on life support. (I know, three metaphors there. Just go with it.)

There were two wars still to fight and, hopefully, resolve. The health insurance system was a holy mess, and with people being thrown out of work by the hundreds of thousands, the pool of Americans without any coverage at all was expanding rather than shrinking.

I could go on.

Given these enormous challenges, what could one reasonably expect from a President Obama?

> In the short term he has to be more of a medic than a superman.

When Franklin D. Roosevelt took office in March 1933, with the country all but paralyzed by the Depression, he delivered an upbeat inaugural address famous for its assertion about fearing "fear itself." Less poetic but more to the point was his frank acknowledgement that "our primary task is to put people to work."

So it is with Barack Obama. Above all else, he has to stop the hemorrhaging of employment in the United States and stabilize the economy. In the short term he has to be more of a medic than a superman. The economic wounds are deep, and there is no guarantee that Obama can return the country to a period of substantial growth and prosperity in the near future. Even Roosevelt was unable to end the Depression; that didn't occur until World War II.

But if Obama can stop the bleeding, if he can stabilize the economy and ease some of the pain of joblessness and foreclosures, he will have racked up a real achievement.

There is, however, another crucially important task for the president-elect, one which Roosevelt also succinctly described at his first inaugural. "This," said Roosevelt, "is pre-eminently the time to speak the truth, the whole truth, frankly and boldly."

Over the past several years, Americans have been lied to, conned, defrauded and generally let down in every way imaginable by their government leaders. The truth was as much a casualty as the economy during that stretch. Voters were sold a bill of goods on the multitrillion-dollar Iraq war and they're still waiting, nearly three decades after the election of Ronald Reagan, for the benefits of wholesale deregulation and tax cuts for the rich to trickle down to the men and women struggling to maintain a modest middle-class standard of living.

Obama campaigned on a mantra of change. The way to follow through on that is for him to be a relentlessly honest voice in the White House, in good times and bad.

Rebuilding the American economy will take time. Winding down two wars while protecting the nation against the evils of terror and other threats will require years of enormous effort. But a President Obama can be honest with the American people from Day 1.

And from that honesty comes the logical next step — a president inviting ordinary Americans to take a more active part in the civic and political affairs of the nation.

There is so much to do. If Obama will level with the public and ask for the help not just of politicians and business people and academics, but of ordinary men and women (and children) in the great and consuming adventure of reviving a stricken nation, the payoff will likely be huge.

Obama was born the year Jack Kennedy asked a new generation of Americans to "ask not" what their country could do for them. And he pushed that theme last May when he filled in for Ted Kennedy as the commencement speaker at Wesleyan University.

Obama urged the graduates to consider how they might participate more fully in the civic life and public affairs of the nation. He made it sound exciting. "It's only when you hitch your wagon to something larger than yourself," he said, "that you realize your true potential and discover the role you'll play in writing the next great chapter in America's story."

He added, "There are so many ways to serve and so much need at this defining moment in our history."

That is the message the nation needs to hear from Obama on the day he steps into the White House. It would take the question of what to expect from a President Obama off the table, and replace it with the challenge of what we should expect from ourselves. ♦

Addressing a crowd in St. Louis. October 17, 2008.

The new First Family on stage in Chicago. November 4, 2008.

CHAPTER FIVE

VICTORY

"If there's anyone out there who still doubts that America is a place where all things are possible; who still questions the power of our democracy, tonight is your answer."

NOVEMBER 4, 2008

W

HEN SENATOR BARACK OBAMA stepped from his plane on the final ride of his presidential candidacy and loped to the bottom of the stairs, he did something he had not done at the end of any of the thousands of miles logged on this journey.

He saluted.

A group of his campaign workers had gathered at Midway Airport in Chicago to watch him arrive from his last trip, a short hop from nearby Indiana. Given the day, as Obama raised his hand to offer his gratitude, it looked a lot like a gesture from a commander in chief.

When he went to vote with Michelle and their two daughters on Tuesday morning, he had narrowly missed another familiar face at his polling place. Bill Ayers, the former member of the radical Weather Underground who became a central figure in the attacks from John McCain and Sarah Palin, had voted there a few minutes earlier.

In the final hours of a 22-month campaign, Obama quickly moved on to an election day tradition that is rooted in a sweaty superstition: basketball. Twice in his primary fight with Hillary Rodham Clinton he skipped his afternoon game on the day ballots were cast. And both times he lost.

So at 2:45 p.m. Obama arrived at a gymnasium on the West Side, aptly named Attack Athletics. For two hours, he ran up and down the court with Senator Bob Casey, Democrat of Pennsylvania, who had become a good friend, along with a close group of Chicago pals who assembled to help take his mind off the other events of the day.

"We are all very superstitious about how things are," said Dr. Eric Whitaker, a friend who traveled with Obama for the final days of the race. "When he lost in New Hampshire and Las Vegas we didn't play, so we've not missed an election day since."

Senator Barack Obama on Election Day in Chicago. November 4, 2008.

Voters line up at P.S. 375 as the polls open in Brooklyn, N.Y. November 4, 2008.

Seventy-nine-year-old rancher Bill Pinkerton leaves the one-room Beaver Creek Schoolhouse in rural Treasure County after voting in Missoula, Mont. November 4, 2008.

DRYERS

Casting a ballot at the Su Nuevo Laundromat in Chicago. November 4, 2008.

"The day shimmered with history as voters began lining up before dark — hours before polls opened — to take part in the culmination of a campaign that, over the course of two years, commanded an extraordinary amount of attention from the American public."

— From "Obama Wins Election" by Adam Nagourney, The New York Times, November 4, 2008

Pre-dawn voter lineup in Vienna, Va. November 4, 2008.

It was a reprieve — perhaps the final one for a while — with no reporters and no cheering crowds. The candidate stepped out to take a phone call or two, but otherwise there were no interruptions that would have punctuated an ordinary day on the road.

Friends tried to keep Obama, still grieving over the death two days before of the grandmother who helped raise him, surrounded by familiar Chicago faces.

By nightfall, thousands of his admirers had streamed into Grant Park for the celebration. At a nearby hotel, he took one more pass through his speech, while commentary about his future played on television sets in the background.

Celebrities, including Oprah Winfrey, gathered in a tent to await his arrival.

> ## *By nightfall, thousands of his admirers had streamed into Grant Park for the celebration.*

As Ohio was called for Obama, a roar sounded from the 125,000 people gathered in Hutchison Field in Grant Park. It was the last state needed to put Obama over the top. But the networks waited to make their calls until 11 p.m., Eastern time, when polls closed in California and the West Coast. The candidate waited to watch McCain's gracious concession speech, in which he praised the president-elect as a fellow American and paid homage to the racial barrier just fallen.

"This is a historic election, and I recognize the significance it has for African-Americans and for the special pride that must be theirs tonight," McCain said, adding, "We both realize that we have come a long way from the injustices that once stained our nation's reputation."

Finally, appearing a bit exhausted, Barack Obama stood at the lectern, looking over a vast undulating sea of screaming humanity of all races, waving American flags. "What a scene, what a crowd," he said, shaking his head. "Wow." He took a long drink out of the water bottle inside the lectern.

Senator John McCain conceding the election and calming supporters with his running mate, Sarah Palin, at his side in Phoenix, Ariz. November 4, 2008.

STEPHEN CROWLEY/NYT

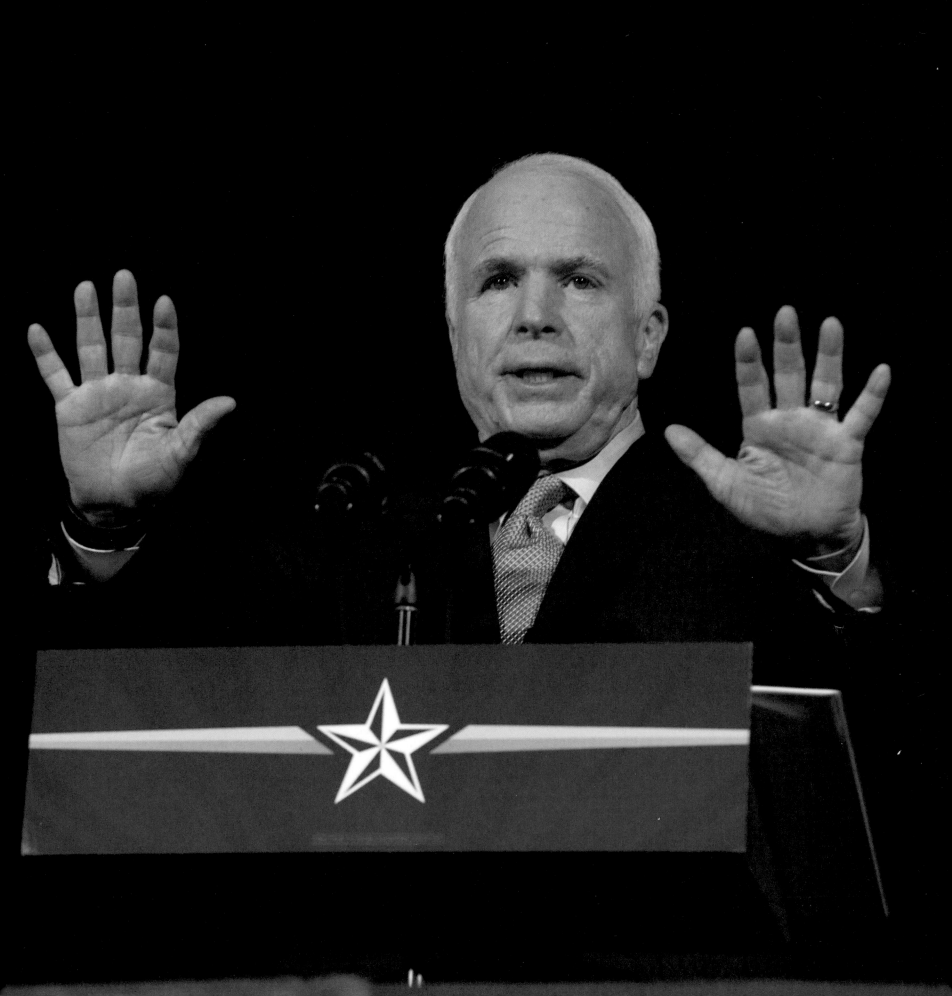

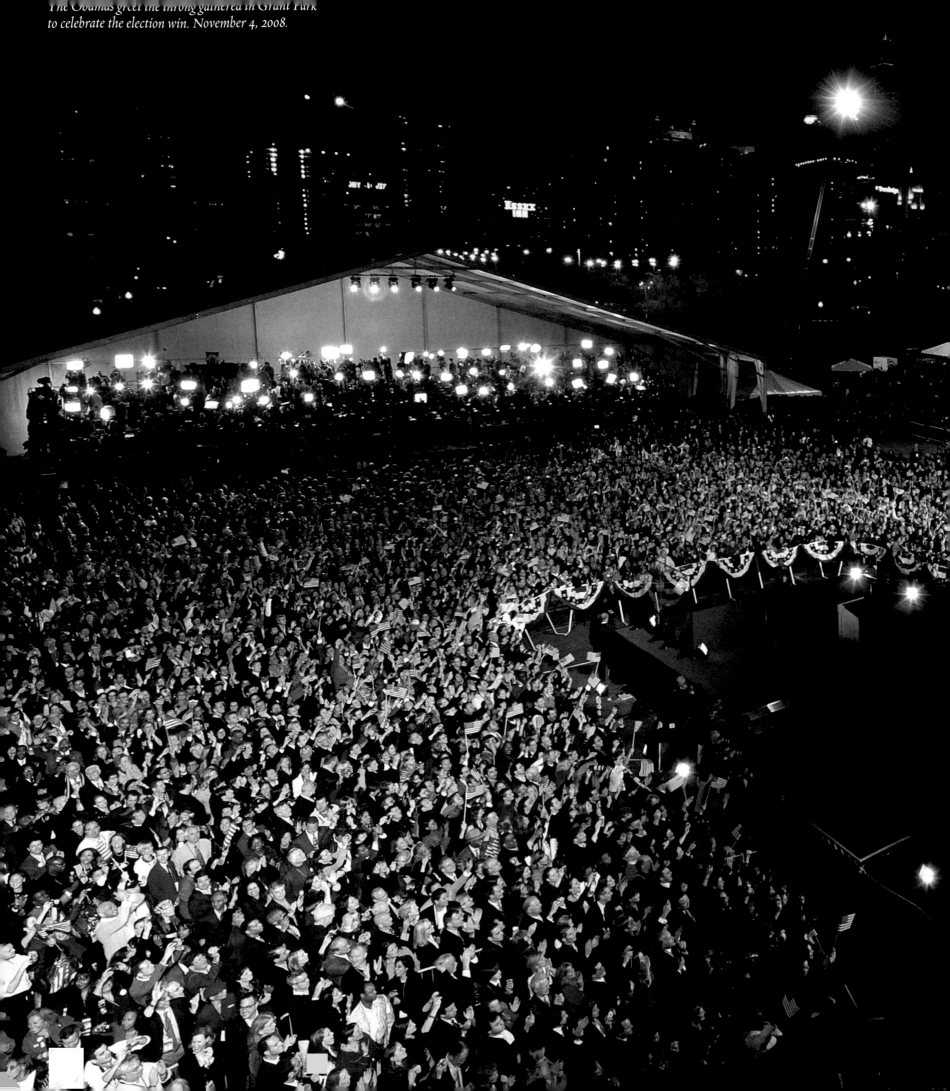

The Obamas greet the throng gathered in Grant Park to celebrate the election win. November 4, 2008.

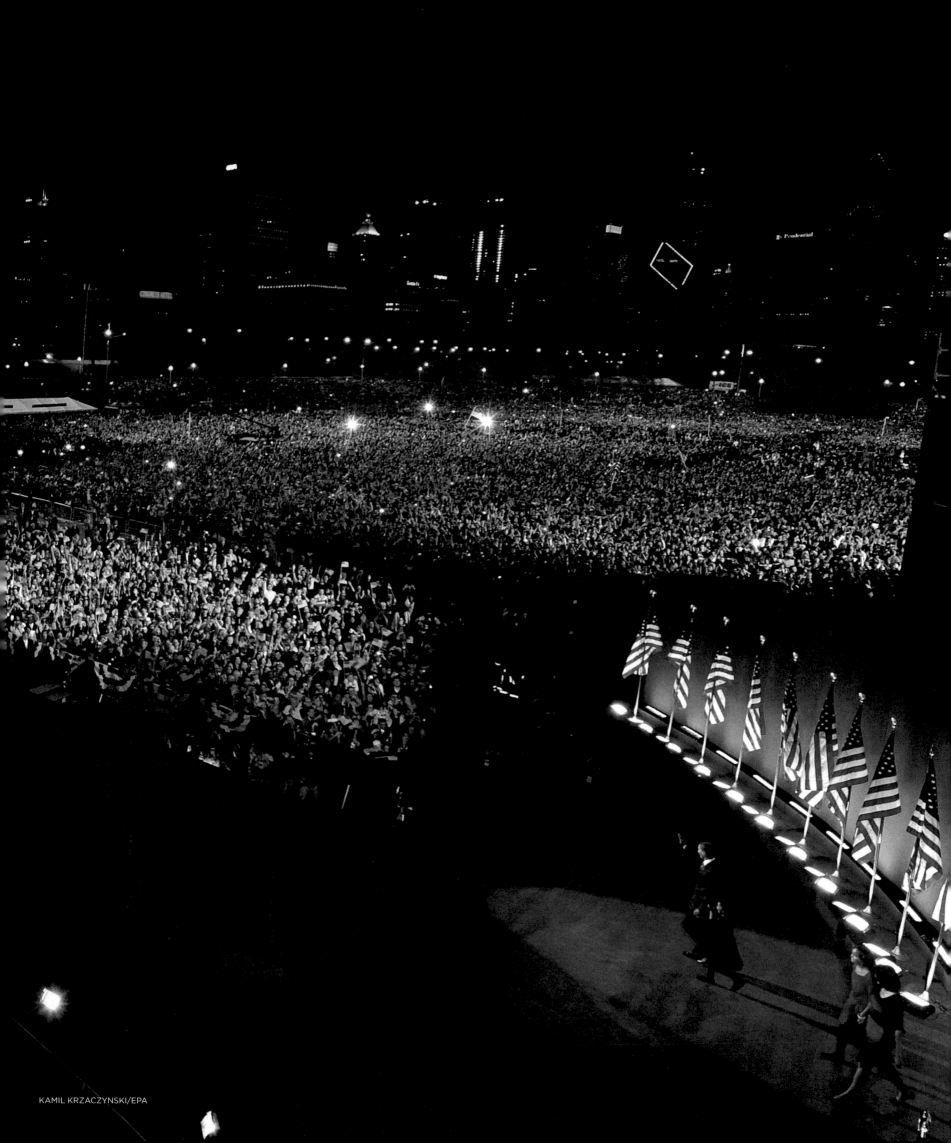

"For that is the true genius of America — that America can change. Our union can be perfected. And what we have already achieved gives us hope for what we can and must achieve tomorrow."

—*November 4, 2008*

With a bank of flags at his back, he told the screaming, dancing crowd, "If there is anyone out there who still doubts that America is a place where all things are possible, who still wonders if the dream of our founders is alive in our time, who still questions the power of our democracy, tonight is your answer."

"It's been a long time coming," the president-elect added, "but tonight, because of what we did on this date in this election at this defining moment, change has come to America."

Not only had he captured the presidency, but he also led his party to sharp gains in Congress. This put Democrats in control of the House, the Senate and the White House for the first time since 1995, when Bill Clinton was in office.

> *"It's been a long time coming," the president-elect added, "but tonight, because of what we did on this date in this election at this defining moment, change has come to America."*

Spontaneous parties erupted on streets across America. At 2 a.m., about 20 revelers from Times Square congregated outside The New York Times's new headquarters on Eighth Avenue, waiting for newspapers to mark the historic occasion. When a senior editor appeared with a bundle of early editions, the crowd went nuts and began taking her picture holding the newspaper with the simple headline that captured their joy: OBAMA.

Oceans away in Jakarta, a young Indonesian student, attending the same public school where Obama's mother had sent him, was hoisted aloft on the shoulders of his joyous schoolmates, waving his shirt in the air. It was a picture repeated elsewhere around the globe, especially in Kenya, where some members of Obama's more distant family made plans to attend the inauguration.

At Obama headquarters in Albany, Georgia, where as a part of the nascent civil rights movement she had been beaten back with tear gas and billy clubs, Rutha Mae Harris could not hold back her tears any longer, the emotions of a lifetime released in a flood.

"Glory, glory, hallelujah," she sang. ♦

The Obamas and the Bidens celebrate victory. November 4, 2008.

DOUG MILLS/NYT

ELECTION NIGHT

NOVEMBER 4, 2008

I f there is anyone out there who still doubts that America is a place where all things are possible; who still wonders if the dream of our founders is alive in our time; who still questions the power of our democracy, tonight is your answer.

It's the answer told by lines that stretched around schools and churches in numbers this nation has never seen; by people who waited three hours and four hours, many for the very first time in their lives, because they believed that this time must be different; that their voice could be that difference.

It's the answer spoken by young and old, rich and poor, Democrat and Republican, black, white, Latino, Asian, Native American, gay, straight, disabled and not disabled — Americans who sent a message to the world that we have never been a collection of red states and blue states: we are, and always will be, the United States of America.

It's the answer that led those who have been told for so long by so many to be cynical, and fearful, and doubtful of what we can achieve to put their hands on the arc of history and bend it once more toward the hope of a better day.

DAMON WINTER/NYT

It's been a long time coming, but tonight, because of what we did on this day, in this election, at this defining moment, change has come to America.

I just received a very gracious call from Senator McCain. He fought long and hard in this campaign, and he's fought even longer and harder for the country he loves. He has endured sacrifices for America that most of us cannot begin to imagine, and we are better off for the service rendered by this brave and selfless leader. I congratulate him and Governor Palin for all they have achieved, and I look forward to working with them to renew this nation's promise in the months ahead.

I want to thank my partner in this journey, a man who campaigned from his heart and spoke for the men and women he grew up with on the streets of Scranton and rode with on that train home to Delaware, the vice president-elect of the United States, Joe Biden.

I would not be standing here tonight without the unyielding support of my best friend for the last 16 years, the rock of our family and the love of my life, our nation's next first lady, Michelle Obama. Sasha and Malia, I love you both so much, and you have earned the new puppy that's coming with us to the White House. And while she's no longer with us, I know my grandmother is watching, along with the family that made me who I am. I miss them tonight, and know that my debt to them is beyond measure.

To my campaign manager, David Plouffe, my chief strategist, David Axelrod, and the best campaign team ever assembled in the history of politics — you made this happen, and I am forever grateful for what you've sacrificed to get it done.

But above all, I will never forget who this victory truly belongs to — it belongs to you.

I was never the likeliest candidate for this office. We didn't start with much money or many endorsements. Our campaign was not hatched in the halls of Washington — it began in the backyards of Des Moines and the living rooms of Concord and the front porches of Charleston.

It was built by working men and women who dug into what little savings they had to give five dollars and ten dollars and twenty dollars to this cause. It grew strength from the young people who rejected the myth of their generation's apathy; who left their homes and their families for jobs that offered little pay and less sleep; from the not-so-young people who braved the bitter cold and scorching heat to knock on the doors of perfect strangers; from the millions of Americans who volunteered, and organized, and proved that more than two centuries later, a government of the people, by the people and for the people has not perished from this Earth. This is your victory.

I know you didn't do this just to win an election and I know you didn't do it for me. You did it because you understand the enormity of the task that lies ahead. For even as we celebrate tonight, we know the challenges that tomorrow will bring are the greatest of our lifetime — two wars, a planet in peril, the worst financial crisis in a century. Even as we stand here tonight, we know there are brave Americans waking up in the deserts of Iraq and the mountains of Afghanistan to risk their lives for us. There are mothers and fathers who will lie awake after their children fall asleep and wonder how they'll make the mortgage, or pay their doctor's bills, or save enough for college. There is new energy to harness and new jobs to be created; new schools to build and threats to meet and alliances to repair.

The road ahead will be long. Our climb will be steep. We may not get there in one year or even one term, but America — I have never been more hopeful than I am tonight that we will get there. I promise you — we as a people will get there.

There will be setbacks and false starts. There are many who won't agree with every decision or policy I make as president, and we know that government can't solve every problem. But I will always be honest with you about the challenges we face. I will listen to you, especially when we disagree. And above all, I will ask you join in the work of remaking this nation the only way it's been done in America for 221 years — block by block, brick by brick, calloused hand by calloused hand.

What began 21 months ago in the depths of winter must not end on this autumn night. This victory alone is not the change we seek — it is only the chance for us to make that change. And that cannot happen if we go back to the way things were. It cannot happen without you.

So let us summon a new spirit of patriotism; of service and responsibility where each of us resolves to pitch in and work harder and look after not only ourselves, but each other. Let us remember that if this financial crisis taught us anything, it's that we cannot have a thriving Wall Street while Main Street suffers — in this country, we rise or fall as one nation; as one people.

Let us resist the temptation to fall back on the same partisanship and pettiness and immaturity that has poisoned our politics for so long. Let us remember that it was a man from this state who first carried the banner of the Republican Party to the White House — a party founded on the values of self-reliance, individual liberty, and national unity. Those are values we all share, and while the Democratic Party has won a great victory tonight, we do so with a measure of humility and determination to heal the divides that have held back our progress. As Lincoln said to a nation far more divided than ours, "We are not enemies, but friends . . . though passion may have strained it must not break our bonds of affection." And to those Americans whose support I have yet to earn — I may not have won your vote, but I hear your voices, I need your help, and I will be your president too.

And to all those watching tonight from beyond our shores, from parliaments and palaces to those who are huddled around radios in the forgotten corners of our world — our stories are singular, but our destiny is shared, and a new dawn of American leadership is at hand. To those who would tear this world down — we will defeat you. To those who seek peace and security — we support you. And to all those who have wondered if America's beacon still burns as bright — tonight we proved once more that the true strength of our nation comes not from the might of our arms or the scale of our wealth, but from the enduring power of our ideals: democracy, liberty, opportunity and unyielding hope.

For that is the true genius of America — that America can change. Our union can be perfected. And what we have already achieved gives us hope for what we can and must achieve tomorrow.

This election had many firsts and many stories that will be told for generations. But one that's on my mind tonight is about a woman who cast her ballot in Atlanta. She's a lot like the millions of others who stood in line to make their voice heard in this election except for one thing — Ann Nixon Cooper is 106 years old.

She was born just a generation past slavery; a time when there were no cars on the road or planes in the sky; when someone like her couldn't vote for two reasons — because she was a woman and because of the color of her skin.

And tonight, I think about all that she's seen throughout her century in America — the heartache and the hope; the struggle and the progress; the times we were told that we can't, and the people who pressed on with that American creed: Yes we can.

At a time when women's voices were silenced and their hopes dismissed, she lived to see them stand up and speak out and reach for the ballot. Yes we can.

When there was despair in the dust bowl and depression across the land, she saw a nation conquer fear itself with a New Deal, new jobs and a new sense of common purpose. Yes we can.

When the bombs fell on our harbor and tyranny threatened the world, she was there to witness a generation rise to greatness and a democracy was saved. Yes we can.

She was there for the buses in Montgomery, the hoses in Birmingham, a bridge in Selma and a preacher from Atlanta who told a people that "We Shall Overcome." Yes we can.

A man touched down on the moon, a wall came down in Berlin, a world was connected by our own science and imagination. And this year, in this election, she touched her finger to a screen, and cast her vote, because after 106 years in America, through the best of times and the darkest of hours, she knows how America can change. Yes we can.

America, we have come so far. We have seen so much. But there is so much more to do. So tonight, let us ask ourselves — if our children should live to see the next century; if my daughters should be so lucky to live as long as Ann Nixon Cooper, what change will they see? What progress will we have made?

This is our chance to answer that call. This is our moment. This is our time — to put our people back to work and open doors of opportunity for our kids; to restore prosperity and promote the cause of peace; to reclaim the American Dream and reaffirm that fundamental truth — that out of many, we are one; that while we breathe, we hope, and where we are met with cynicism, and doubt, and those who tell us that we can't, we will respond with that timeless creed that sums up the spirit of a people:

Yes We Can. Thank you, God bless you and may God bless the United States of America. ◆

> **B**ut above all, I will never forget who this victory truly belongs to — it belongs to you.

Tears of joy in Grant Park as CNN projects Barack Obama the winner of the presidential race. November 4, 2008.

Celebration in the streets of Harlem, New York City. November 5, 2008.

"African-Americans wept and danced in the streets on Tuesday night, declaring that a once-reluctant nation had finally lived up to its democratic promise. Strangers of all colors exulted in small towns and big cities. And white voters marveled at what they had wrought in turning a page on the country's bitter racial history."

—From *"Vaulting the Racial Divide, Obama Persuaded Americans to Follow"* by Rachel L. Swarns, The New York Times, November 5, 2008

Students from an Islamic high school in New Delhi, India, pose near a wooden cut-out of Barack Obama after learning he was elected the 44th president of the United States. November 5, 2008.

RUTH FREMSON/NYT

French and Americans cheer the election results outside a bar in Paris. November 5, 2008.

OLIVIER LABAN-MATTEI/AFP/GETTY

At the president-elect's former school in Jakarta, students display his picture. November 5, 2008.

In his rendering, Palestinian artist Walid Ayoub envisions President-elect Obama holding peace symbols. The drawing is exhibited next to others of late Palestinian leader Yasser Arafat and Jesus in Ramallah, West Bank. November 5, 2008.

INSIDE THE TIMES

Planning for the election issue of The New York Times began weeks before the voting.

The political team of editors and reporters had to be ready, on tight deadlines, to deal with either an Obama or McCain victory. They had assigned a battery of stories based on both outcomes.

Network exit polls, expected at 5 p.m., would help the journalists sort out some of the voting trends, but only real votes would permit editors to begin calling the results as polls began to close.

It's hard to describe the excitement in the newsroom on election night. The third floor, where the political team had its hub and the desk for NYTimes.com was located, was positively humming. Journalists from other parts of the paper gathered just to be near the action.

But the daytime hours, before the polls closed, could seem like an eternity. "What's the turnout?" everyone asked and the only answers came in anecdotal shards from the polling places where Times reporters and photographers had been assigned across the country.

At noon, Managing Editor Jill Abramson headed to a traditional Election Day lunch at The Palm steakhouse in midtown Manhattan. For her, this was part ritual and part reunion with other reporters and network correspondents who had covered national elections for decades. Abramson's career had begun in 1976, when she helped cover the New Hampshire primaries for Time when she was a student at Harvard.

This was the same lunch, four years earlier, when notoriously faulty exit polls had begun circulating. Tom Brokaw had jotted down the absurdly wrong state-by-state results being dictated over his cellphone. When even South Carolina showed a Kerry edge, Brokaw insisted the exit poll looked fishy. Still, the exit polls had cast a pall over the Bush campaign and set some false expectations for the early returns. This year, cellphones and BlackBerrys had been confiscated from the few analysts allowed to see the early wave of exit polls and there were no leaks.

Executive Editor Bill Keller, Abramson and John Geddes, The Times's other managing editor, knew they were publishing a newspaper for the ages. In the event of an Obama win, they had assigned three anchor articles for the front page, besides the traditional "lede-all" news story to be written by Adam Nagourney, The Times's chief political correspondent. The three articles touched on the themes of race, the enormity of the economic problems facing Obama and the new face he would show to the rest of the world.

Keller had thought of an untraditional headline: OBAMA. No

Even though The Times had printed several hundred thousand extra papers, the entire city was sold out.

verb, nothing else. It was a brilliant idea, applauded even by the most tradition-bound journalists at The Times.

As the battleground states began falling for Obama, Abramson entered Nagourney's writing chamber to read a draft of his beautifully rendered lead news story. They tinkered, just a bit, with the first sentence. Then Nagourney hit the send button:

"Barack Hussein Obama was elected the 44th president of the United States on Tuesday, sweeping away the last racial barrier in American politics with ease as the country chose him as its first black chief executive.

"The election of Barack Obama amounted to a national catharsis — a repudiation of a historically unpopular Republican president and his economic and foreign policies, and an embrace of Mr. Obama's call for a change in the direction and the tone of the country.

"But it was just as much a strikingly symbolic moment in the evolution of the nation's fraught racial history, a breakthrough that would have seemed unthinkable just two years ago."

Once the layout of the front page had been designed and the headline chosen, Keller had one more crucial call: the front page photograph. Michele McNally, The Times's editor of photography, brought him her two favorites, one shot by Doug Mills, another by Damon Winter. One was a close-in portrait of the president-elect at the moment of victory, the other a joyous quartet of Barack, Michelle, Malia and Sasha.

They mulled. Keller consulted Abramson and Geddes. Both pictures were superb. Mock-ups of front pages with each picture were prepared and compared. Now Keller was certain: the group shot, featuring America's new first family, told the story perfectly.

Because the results were clear by 11 p.m., the editors' work was much speedier than in previous election nights. Keller, Abramson and Geddes had all been in the newsroom on election night 2000, when Joe Lelyveld, then executive editor, called out "Stop the Presses!" in the wee hours of the morning when Florida could not be called. This time, there were no glitches, no surprises.

The first printed papers arrived in the newsroom around 1:30 a.m. A crowd had gathered in front of the building to get the first copies off the presses. By the time the editors returned the next morning, a line had formed and snaked down the block. Even though The Times had printed several hundred thousand extra papers, the entire city was sold out. More press runs were added. By Friday, when the lines began to abate, The Times had sold approximately 25,000 election papers at its headquarters alone.

This version was never published. The above image was from a proof intended for a 10:30 p.m. closing time that was pulled at about 10:15 p.m. At the time the race was too close to call, shown by the large photos of both candidates and a headline expressing Obama's lead.

For an 11:15 p.m. postcript (re-plating presses between standard editions), The Times introduced the three essays planned in the event of an Obama win.

For the close of the second edition, at 12:30 p.m., The Times substituted the photo of Obama landing in Chicago earlier in the day with a photo of Obama and his family at the victory rally in Grant Park.

For Much of the Country, a Sizeable Shift

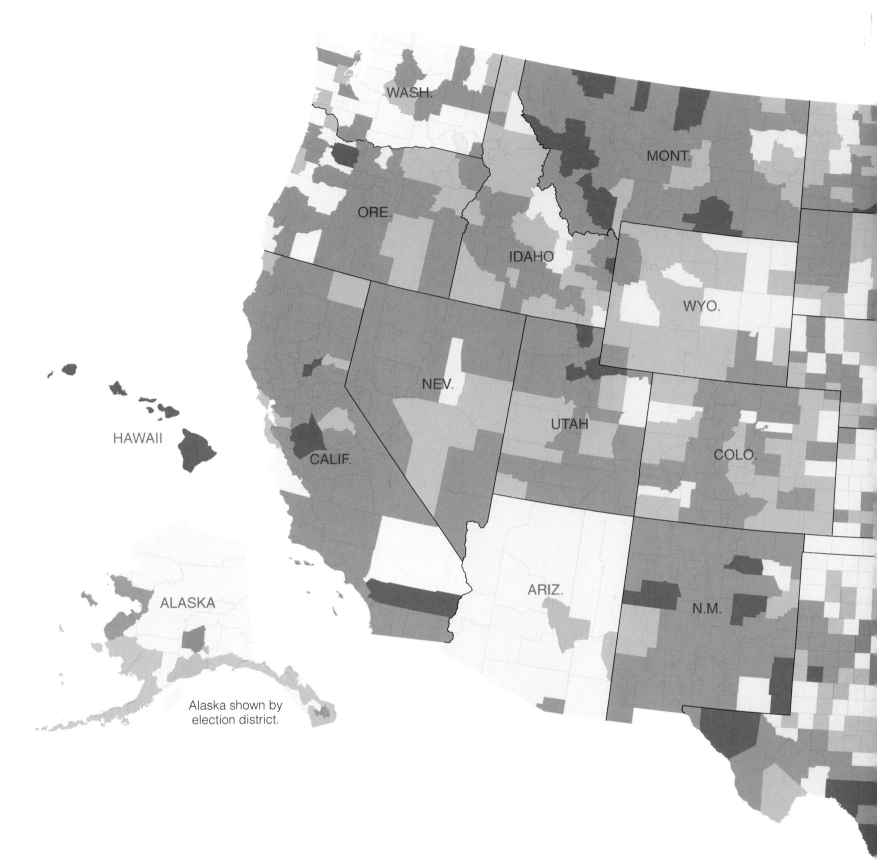

Alaska shown by
election district.

The Republican West

Even strongly Republican states like **Idaho** and **Utah** took large steps toward the Democratic side. John McCain won Salt Lake County, Utah, but by just 2,000 votes. President Bush had carried it by 80,000 votes.

Northern High Plains

Barack Obama was familiar to voters in **North Dakota** and **Montana** after the primaries. He held 11 events in Montana and had a large field operation from the primary that was retained for the general election.

Rural and Urban Texas

Big cities moved in large numbers to Mr. Obama, providing a sharp contrast here between urban and rural voters. Mr. Obama won Dallas County, a place that Mr. Bush won in 2004 by 125,000 votes.

Rio Grande Valley

Hispanics in the southern tip of **Texas**, who had shown affinity for Mr. Bush in past elections, shifted to the Democratic side. Mr. Obama gained votes from Hispanics who favored Hillary Rodham Clinton in the primaries.

Indiana

Much of the state shifted away from Republicans, but the move was most noticeable in rural counties that had kept the state reliably red in previous elections.

White Southern Counties

Rural white counties from **Kentucky** to **Texas** took a different tack from the rest of the country, moving strongly toward Mr. McCain. Turnout in 90-percent-white counties in **Tennessee** and **Arkansas** was barely changed from 2004.

Blacks in the South

Black voters flooded to the polls in rural counties from **Virginia** to **Mississippi**. In **Alabama**, a safely Republican redoubt, turnout in majority-black counties was up 15 percent.

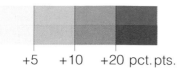

Compared with 2004, county voted more ...

DEMOCRATIC
REPUBLICAN

+5 +10 +20 pct. pts.

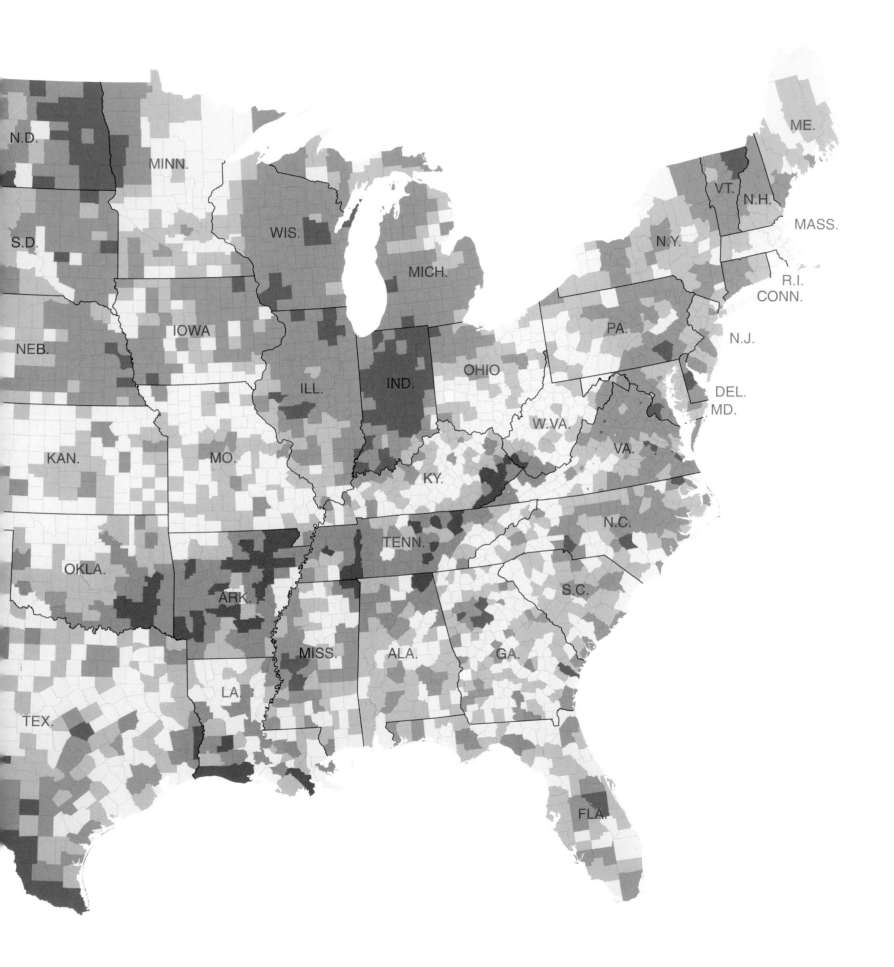

ARCHIE TSE/NYT

Thinking of Good Vibrations

GAIL COLLINS

Tralalalalala.

We are only thinking cheerful thoughts today, people. America did good. Enjoy.

Even if you voted for John McCain, be happy. You've got the best of all worlds. Today, you can bask in the realization that there are billions of people around the planet who loathed our country last week but are now in awe of its capacity to rise above historic fears and prejudices, that once again, the United States will have a president the world wants to follow.

Then later, when things get screwed up, you can point out that it's not your fault.

About the inevitable disasters: I am sorry to tell you, excited youth of America, that Barack Obama is going to make mistakes. And the country's broke. Perhaps we should have mentioned this before. But let's leave all that to 2009. When somebody runs one of the best presidential campaigns ever, he deserves a little time to enjoy the sweet spot between achievement of a goal and the arrival of the consequences.

Let's hear it for the voters. Good turnout, guys — especially you Virginians who stood in line for seven hours. A professor at George Mason University who studies this sort of thing claims that there hasn't been such a high participation level since 1908. You could turn out to be the ever-elusive answer to the question: "Name one thing that Barack Obama has in common with William Howard Taft?"

Let's hear it for Hillary Clinton, who lost but made the country comfortable with the idea of a woman as chief executive. And Joe Biden, who actually ran a disciplined campaign, given his truly exceptional capacity to say weird things.

....

Let's hear it for the voters. Good turnout, guys — especially you Virginians who stood in line for seven hours.

....

And let's give a shout-out to John McCain. As desperate as he was, he still passed up opportunities to poke hard at the nation's fault lines of race, religion and region — although he has probably created a permanent gap between the rest of us and segments of the country who feel under imminent threat from Bill Ayers.

McCain ran a dreadful campaign, but it's over. Give the guy a break. He was stuck with George Bush. And the Republican Party. And the fact that he was constitutionally incapable of giving a decent speech. The road was hard, but he soldiered on and did a lovely concession Tuesday night. Kudos.

Sarah Palin did go over the top with her small towns vs. the world mantra. However, she does get credit for giving us a real understanding of the difference between a moose and a caribou.

O.K., there is nothing positive to say about Sarah Palin. And Alaska, are you re-electing Ted Stevens? What's going on there? Did you actually believe him when he said that the court verdict was still up in the air? On the day after he was found guilty? By the way, if Stevens does win, it will be with about 106,000 votes. In total. There are more people than that in my immediate neighborhood! What kind of state is this, anyway?

But we're in a good mood, so let's forget Alaska. Instead, we'll contemplate the fact that North Carolina tossed Elizabeth Dole out of office despite her ad campaign aimed at convincing the state that her opponent, Kay Hagan, was an atheist. This was accomplished, you may remember, through the creative strategy of showing Hagan's picture along with another woman's voice saying: "There is no God!" If Dole had won, by the next election we would have been bombarded

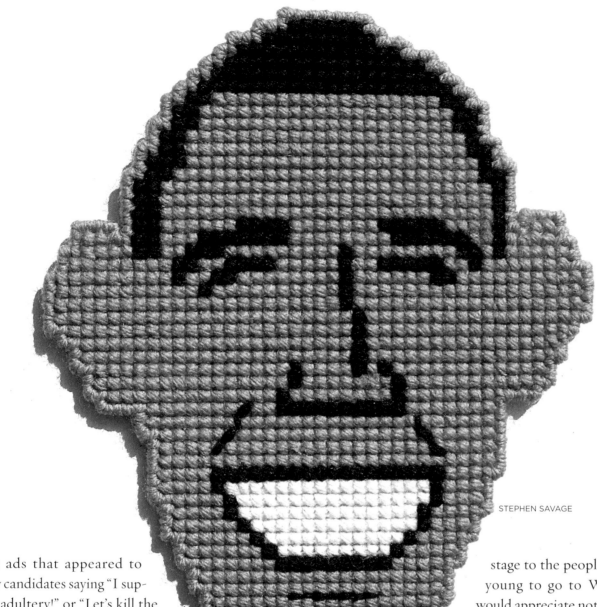

STEPHEN SAVAGE

with ads that appeared to show candidates saying "I support adultery!" or "Let's kill the puppies!" Now that won't happen. Thank you, North Carolina.

By the way, I believe that during the campaign McCain's great friend Senator Lindsey Graham said something along the line of promising to drown himself if North Carolina went for Obama. I believe I speak for us all, Senator Graham, when I say that we are feeling extremely mellow today and you do not have to follow through.

Congratulations to Senator Susan Collins on her re-election. The entire moderate Republican caucus in the Senate may now wind up consisting of women from Maine. As Maine goes, so go the Supreme Court nominations.

Finally, on behalf of the baby-boom generation, I would like to hear a little round of applause before we cede the stage to the people who were too young to go to Woodstock and would appreciate not having to listen to the stories about it anymore. It looks as though we will be represented in history by only two presidents, one of whom is George W. Bush. Bummer.

The boomers didn't win any wars and that business about being self-involved was not entirely unfounded. On the other hand, they made the nation get serious about the idea of everybody being created equal. And now American children are going to grow up unaware that there's anything novel in an African-American president or a woman running for the White House.

We'll settle for that. ♦

The New York Times, November 5, 2008

Outgoing and incoming presidents enter the White House. November 10, 2008.

DOUG MILLS/NYT

CHAPTER SIX

TIME OF TRANSITION

"And to those Americans whose support I have yet to earn: I may not have won your vote tonight, but I hear your voices, I need your help and I will be your president, too."

NOVEMBER 4, 2008

DAMON WINTER/NYT

THE FINANCIAL TSUNAMI WAS GAINING such ferocity that virtually every large institution, from investment banks to insurers to companies like Citigroup, was approaching Washington for federal funds. Help couldn't wait.

Although Barack Obama kept reminding people that the United States only had one president at a time, he knew the world expected him to get to work to help stabilize the teetering economy. That meant the quick announcement of an economic team and a fiscal stimulus plan, perhaps one as large as $700 billion, equivalent to the financial bailout plan approved by the Congress before the election.

For his first staff announcements, the president-elect turned to two old Clinton hands, Representative Rahm Emanuel of Illinois and John Podesta.

The new Treasury secretary was Timothy F. Geithner, the young president of the Federal Reserve Bank of New York. Former Treasury Secretary Lawrence H. Summers was to be the director of the National Economic Council in the White House, the president's principal economic adviser and policy coordinator.

For his national security team, Obama also went long on experience. The biggest surprise was Hillary Rodham Clinton for secretary of state. Although they had disagreed about the Iraq war and during the primaries Clinton had portrayed herself as more hawkish than Obama, she opted to accept the chance to play on the world stage once again.

Obama asked Bush's defense secretary, Robert M. Gates, to stay on and picked Gen. James L. Jones, the former NATO commander and Marine Corps commandant, to be national security adviser. Another former rival for the Democratic nomination, Bill Richardson of New Mexico, was chosen for Commerce secretary, but later withdrew. Arizona's Janet Napolitano was selected as secretary of Homeland Security. All were expected to be approved by Congress.

The staff also included campaign hands like David Axelrod, who would keep his portfolio on message and communications, Robert Gibbs, the press secretary, and Chicago loyalists like Valerie Jarrett.

At his first press conference, President-elect Obama, followed by Vice President-elect Biden, introduced his economic team, Chicago. November 7, 2008.

DOUG MILLS/NYT

The once and future couples at the White House. November 10, 2008.

For director of the Central Intelligence Agency, the president-elect chose another veteran of both Congress and the Clinton White House, Leon Panetta. The only lingering problems seemed to be the private law clients of the Attorney General-designate, Eric Holder, who was deputy attorney general in the Clinton Justice Department and handled a controversial pardon case in his last days in office.

> *Historians made comparisons to Lincoln, who took office at the beginning of the Civil War, and Roosevelt, who faced the Depression.*

Although his campaign nickname was "No Drama Obama," the choices meant an Obama White House that would brim with big personalities and far more spirited debate than occurred among the largely like-minded advisers who populated President George W. Bush's first term.

Historians made comparisons to Lincoln, who took office at the beginning of the Civil War, and Roosevelt, who faced the Depression. The most overused cliché derived from Doris Kearns Goodwin's book about the Lincoln cabinet, which Obama had read and admired: team of rivals.

Scandal erupted in early December with the arrest of Gov. Rod Blagojevich of Illinois, who was charged by U.S. Attorney Patrick Fitzgerald with numerous counts of corruption and influence-peddling, including the explosive accusation that he tried to put Obama's Senate seat up for sale to the highest bidder.

For the Obama team, the scandal provided an early test. To minimize any connection between him and Blagojevich, Obama ordered an internal review by his lawyers, including the incoming White House counsel Gregory B. Craig. The findings showed that in the days after Obama's election as president, Emanuel suggested to Governor Blagojevich that the Senate seat should be filled by Valerie Jarrett, who decided not to pursue the seat and to serve in a senior White House position.

DOUG MILLS/ NYT

At a meeting of his economic advisers, Washington, D.C. January 6, 2009.

SCOTT OLSON/GETTY IMAGES

Illinois Gov. Rod Blagojevich introduces former Illinois Attorney General Roland Burris as his choice to fill the U.S. Senate seat vacated by Obama, Chicago. December 30, 2008.

The report concluded that Emanuel had as many as six conversations with the governor's office about the Senate vacancy, but that Obama had none. The report said that neither Emanuel, Jarrett nor any other Obama associates had any talks about a deal in which Blagojevich would benefit from appointing someone to the Senate seat. Prosecutors have not implicated Obama or his advisers.

> *With the breakneck speed of appointments, Obama had little time for post-election relaxation.*

Still, the ethical mess swirling around Gov. Blagojevich continued. First, he insisted on filling Obama's vacant Senate seat with a former Illinois state official, Roland W. Burris. Obama and Senate Majority Leader Harry Reid at first said Burris should not be seated because Blagojevich was not fit to make the appointment. But they changed their minds, in part because Senate Democrats needed Burris's vote. Some members of the Congressional Black Caucus also supported Burris, who would be the Senate's only African-American, and he was sworn in on January 15. In the meantime, in early January, Blagojevich was impeached by a vote of the State House of Representatives, setting the stage for a trial in the State Senate.

With the breakneck speed of appointments, Obama had little time for post-election relaxation, although he hit the gym in Chicago for nearly 90 minutes every day. Finally, over the Christmas holiday, the Obamas left for a vacation in Hawaii. But there was sad family business awaiting them: scattering Toot's ashes near the spot where Obama had scattered those of his mother.

These matters were mere distractions considering the deteriorating state of the economy. In January, as the Obamas returned from their holiday in Hawaii, the nation's jobless rate rose to a 16-year high of 7.2 percent. Obama enlarged his stimulus proposal to $775 billion over two years, saying it would save between three and four million jobs. National polls showed that 65 percent of the country supported his leadership, a much higher approval rate than other president-elects enjoyed. Congressional leaders promised to act on the stimulus package in February.

Body English on the 18th green, Kailua, Hawaii. December 29, 2008.

The president-elect stops for chili in his new hometown, Washington, D.C. January 10, 2009.

Four presidents meet to give advice to the new man: George H.W. Bush, Barack Obama, George W. Bush, Bill Clinton and Jimmy Carter. January 7, 2009.

In terms of the economy, Obama stepped fully into the role of president before his inauguration. He met with congressional leaders and, in a somber but commanding tone, gave a major economic address at George Mason University in the Virginia suburbs of Washington. "For every day we wait or point fingers or drag our feet," he warned, "more Americans will lose their jobs, more families will lose their savings, more dreams will be deferred and denied and our nation will sink deeper into a crisis that, at some point, we may not be able to reverse."

The idea was to build public support by mapping out a series of events to explain his economic approach, including long, televised interviews.

> ## *In terms of the economy, Obama stepped fully into the role of president before his inauguration.*

Obama also asked to meet with all of the living presidents at the White House to pick their collective brains. President Bush hosted a White House luncheon for the group, which included Jimmy Carter, George H.W. Bush and Bill Clinton. It was the first such White House gathering since 1981. Clinton, with his uncanny ability to seize the spotlight, looked down at the custom-designed carpet, with its yellow sunburst pattern that Mr. Bush likes to call "optimistic," and exclaimed, in a voice loud enough for the microphones to pick up, "I looooove this rug!"

The Obamas had moved into a suite at the nearby Hay-Adams Hotel so that Malia and Sasha could begin school after the holiday break. Besides a few official photographs of the president-elect seeing Michelle and the girls off to school, the press gave Malia and Sasha the privacy to adjust and make new friends at Sidwell Friends.

There was one more announcement before the family moved into the White House: Marian Robinson, Michelle's mother and a mainstay for the girls all through the campaign, said she would move in with the First Family after all, putting aside, for now, her worries about losing touch with her friends and beloved Chicago. And the closely followed saga of which breed of man's best friend would share the Obama White House narrowed to two: Labradoodle and Portuguese water dog. ◆

RAHM EMANUEL, 49, was born in Chicago. After serving as a senior adviser in the Clinton White House, he was elected to the House of Representatives in 2002. He ran the Democratic Congressional Campaign Committee in 2006 and became chairman of the House Democratic Caucus in 2007. He is Obama's chief of staff.

JOSEPH R. BIDEN JR., 66, the vice president, was elected to the Senate from Delaware in 1972 at 29 and served for 35 years. He sat on the Judiciary Committee and the Foreign Relations Committee. He ran for president in 1988 and again in 2008.

JOHN D. PODESTA, 60, spent seven years working in the Clinton White House, including two as chief of staff. Before that he worked for Senators Tom Daschle and Patrick Leahy. He is the president of the Center for American Progress, a research group that he founded in 2003. He was co-chairman of Obama's transition team.

TOM DASCHLE, 61, the former Senate majority leader from South Dakota, served 8 years in the House and 18 in the Senate. Since 2004 he has been advising and writing on health care policy. He was an early Obama supporter and is secretary of the Department of Health and Human Services and leader of the new White House Office of Health Reform.

PETE ROUSE, 62, was co-chairman of the Obama-Biden transition team. From 1985 to 2004 he was chief of staff to Tom Daschle. He was also chief of staff to Senator Richard Durbin of Illinois when Durbin was in the House. He was Obama's chief of staff in the Senate. He is a senior adviser to the president.

REGGIE LOVE, 26, studied political science at Duke University, where he played football and basketball. He started working for Obama in 2007 as a staff assistant. He became Obama's personal aide in 2008, a position he continues in the White House.

VALERIE JARRETT, 52, has known Barack and Michelle Obama for almost 20 years. After nearly a decade in Chicago city government — as Mayor Richard M. Daley's deputy chief of staff, a planning commissioner and chairwoman of the Chicago Transit Authority — she left in 1995 to work for a real estate developer. She is a senior adviser to the president.

DAVID AXELROD, 53, wrote about politics for The Chicago Tribune before leaving to manage campaigns, beginning with the first Senate run of Paul Simon, the Illinois Democrat. He was a top adviser for Obama's 2004 Senate race and the chief strategist for his presidential campaign. He is a senior adviser to the president.

ROBERT GIBBS, 37, has worked for Obama since 2004, when he became his communications director. For Obama's presidential campaign, he was communications director and a senior adviser, as well as the candidate's constant companion. He has worked for several other campaigns, including John Kerry's 2004 presidential run. He is White House press secretary.

CLOSE COMPANY

Selected portraits of the Obama team by Nadav Kander, originally published in The New York Times Magazine on January 18, 2009.

GREGORY B. CRAIG, 63, was the State Department's director of policy planning under President Clinton and the lead lawyer in Clinton's 1998 impeachment defense. Before that he was a senior defense- and foreign-policy adviser to Senator Edward M. Kennedy. He was one of the earliest supporters of Obama's candidacy and is White House counsel.

SUSAN E. RICE, 44, worked for the Clinton administration for eight years, serving in several positions dealing with national security and African affairs. She was senior foreign-policy adviser to Obama's presidential campaign. She is ambassador to the United Nations, a post that the president plans to make a cabinet-level position.

Senator Hillary Rodham Clinton takes a seat at her confirmation hearing for secretary of state, Washington, D.C. January 13, 2009.

ROSEBUD AND RADIANCE

During Barack Obama's first news conference after the election, the most pressing question was about what kind of hypoallergenic puppy the Obamas planned to get in the White House, a promise they had made to their daughters, Sasha, 7, and Malia, 10. Next, the frenzy turned to what school the girls would attend in Washington.

Happy talk about White House sleepovers during an interview on "60 Minutes" did little to conceal the Obamas' understandable worries over moving their young daughters into the center of First Family mania.

Rosebud and Radiance, as the Secret Service had named them, would be the youngest children to live in the White House since the Kennedys. For the most part, the Obamas had protected the girls during the campaign. Except for photographs of Obama dropping them at school after the election, most public glimpses were confined to the traditional platform shots at the convention and on election night.

Michelle looked at several private schools and chose Sidwell Friends, a nurturing Quaker school that had educated Chelsea Clinton, Al Gore's son and many other children of politicians.

Michelle's mother, Marian, 71, who had helped care for the girls while she campaigned, would be moving to Washington, too.

Michelle told friends she wanted the girls to have as normal a routine as possible. While the White House staff could make her bed, she wanted the girls to make their own.

Obama was a protective father who never missed a teacher conference. He read Harry Potter with Malia and roughhoused with Sasha, the ham of the family. In her convention speech, Michelle recalled him driving home with her and baby Malia so slowly, with so many backward glances at the baby in the backseat, that she feared they would never make it home.

Michelle said she intended to be more of a "Mom-in-Chief" than first lady and picked as her signature issue helping military families.

On "60 Minutes" Obama called the upending of their lives "one of my greatest worries."

"If at the end of four years, just from a personal standpoint, we can say they are who they are — they remain the great joys that they are — and this hasn't created a whole bunch of problems for them, then I think we're going to feel pretty good."

The parents see their children off to their first day of school in Washington. January 5, 2008.

Obama and Biden visit the Supreme Court justices, from left, Chief Justice John Roberts Jr., John Paul Stevens,
Ruth Bader Ginsberg, Clarence Thomas and David Souter, Washington, D.C. January 14, 2009.

The Obama Agenda

PAUL KRUGMAN

Tuesday, Nov. 4, 2008, is a date that will live in fame (the opposite of infamy) forever. If the election of our first African-American president didn't stir you, if it didn't leave you teary-eyed and proud of your country, there's something wrong with you.

But will the election also mark a turning point in the actual substance of policy? Can Barack Obama really usher in a new era of progressive policies? Yes, he can.

Right now, many commentators are urging Mr. Obama to think small. Some make the case on political grounds: America, they say, is still a conservative country, and voters will punish Democrats if they move to the left. Others say that the financial and economic crisis leaves no room for action on, say, health care reform.

Let's hope that Mr. Obama has the good sense to ignore this advice.

About the political argument: Anyone who doubts that we've had a major political realignment should look at what's happened to Congress. After the 2004 election, there were many declarations that we'd entered a long-term, perhaps permanent era of Republican dominance. Since then, Democrats have won back-to-back victories, picking up at least 12 Senate seats and more than 50 House seats. They now have bigger majorities in both houses than the G.O.P. ever achieved in its 12-year reign.

Bear in mind, also, that this year's presidential election was a clear referendum on political philosophies — and the progressive philosophy won.

Maybe the best way to highlight the importance of that fact is to contrast this year's campaign with what happened

> The response to the economic crisis is, in itself, a chance to advance the progressive agenda.

four years ago. In 2004, President Bush concealed his real agenda. He basically ran as the nation's defender against gay married terrorists, leaving even his supporters nonplussed when he announced, soon after the election was over, that his first priority was Social Security privatization. That wasn't what people thought they had been voting for, and the privatization campaign quickly devolved from juggernaut to farce.

This year, however, Mr. Obama ran on a platform of guaranteed health care and tax breaks for the middle class, paid for with higher taxes on the affluent. John McCain denounced his opponent as a socialist and a "redistributor," but America voted for him anyway. That's a real mandate.

What about the argument that the economic crisis will make a progressive agenda unaffordable?

Well, there's no question that fighting the crisis will cost a lot of money. Rescuing the financial system will probably require large outlays beyond the funds already disbursed. And on top of that, we badly need a program of increased government spending to support output and employment. Could next year's federal budget deficit reach $1 trillion? Yes.

But standard textbook economics says that it's O.K., in fact appropriate, to run temporary deficits in the face of a depressed economy. Meanwhile, one or two years of red ink, while it would add modestly to future federal interest expenses, shouldn't stand in the way of a health care plan that, even if quickly enacted into law, probably wouldn't take effect until 2011.

Beyond that, the response to the economic crisis is, in itself, a chance to advance the progressive agenda.

Now, the Obama administration shouldn't emulate the

ANDRÉ CARRILHO

Bush administration's habit of turning anything and everything into an argument for its preferred policies. (Recession? The economy needs help — let's cut taxes on rich people! Recovery? Tax cuts for rich people work — let's do some more!)

But it would be fair for the new administration to point out how conservative ideology, the belief that greed is always good, helped create this crisis. What F.D.R. said in his second inaugural address — "We have always known that heedless self-interest was bad morals; we know now that it is bad economics" — has never rung truer.

And right now happens to be one of those times when the converse is also true, and good morals are good economics. Helping the neediest in a time of crisis, through expanded health and unemployment benefits, is the morally right thing to do; it's also a far more effective form of economic stimulus than cutting the capital gains tax. Providing aid to beleaguered state and local governments, so that they can sustain essential public services, is important for those who depend on those services; it's also a way to avoid job losses and limit the depth of the economy's slump.

So a serious progressive agenda — call it a new New Deal — isn't just economically possible, it's exactly what the economy needs.

The bottom line, then, is that Barack Obama shouldn't listen to the people trying to scare him into being a do-nothing president. He has the political mandate; he has good economics on his side. You might say that the only thing he has to fear is fear itself. ♦

The New York Times, November 7, 2008

President-elect Barack Obama arrives at his inauguration, Washington, D.C. January 20, 2009.

POOL PHOTO BY JIM BOURG

CHAPTER SEVEN

PRESIDENT BARACK HUSSEIN OBAMA

"On this day, we gather because we have chosen hope over fear, unity of purpose over conflict and discord."

JANUARY 20, 2009

The scene on the mall as the new president delivered his inaugural address. January 20, 2009.

E TOOK THE OATH OF OFFICE on the west front of the U.S. Capitol, where slaves had once baked the bricks, sawed the timber and laid the stone for the foundation. He rose to speak, a few minutes after noon, looking out at an ocean of hope, close to two million people gathered across the National Mall, once a slave market, all the way to the Lincoln Memorial, honoring the president who freed the slaves.

From the veterans of the civil rights movement to the teenagers tapping on their iPhones, the new president's speech was far less important than the moment. Many of those who braved the 17-degree chill to swarm onto the mall at daybreak had said they would not believe America would install a black president until they saw and heard him take the oath, even if on a Jumbotron a mile from the event.

That oath-taking was so historic that his inaugural address became larger than its own language, more imbued with meaning than anything he could say.

Lincoln hovered over almost every aspect of the most anticipated inauguration since John F. Kennedy's. The weekend before the inauguration, Barack Obama and his family had stopped to visit the Lincoln Memorial, studying the words carved into the marble. Malia turned to her father and blurted out: "First African-American president. Better be good."

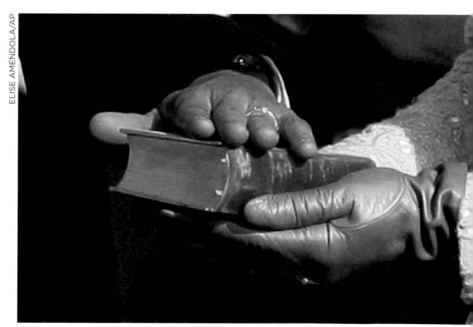

President Obama used Abraham Lincoln's inaugural Bible. January 20, 2009.

The Obamas travel to Washington, D.C., with the Bidens aboard a train. January 17, 2009.

On the president-elect's national day of service, he jokes with a student at Calvin Coolidge High School, Washington, D.C. January 19, 2009.

As he swore to uphold the Constitution, Obama's hand rested on the velvet-covered Bible that Lincoln used in 1861. The china for the inaugural lunch was a replica of a Lincoln set. As he pored over draft after draft of his speech, Obama had re-read Lincoln's collected writings in an attempt to evoke "a larger, fundamental element of American life — the enduring belief that we can constantly remake ourselves to fit our larger dreams," as he had written in a 2005 essay published in Time magazine.

The daunting reality of becoming president seemed to settle on Obama the Sunday before the inauguration. He stood on the steps of the Lincoln Memorial and looked out at a cheering crowd of 400,000 that stretched all the way to the Washington Monument, gathered for a concert and the opening inaugural ceremonies. Speaking as the white marble Lincoln looked down on him, Obama gave somber remarks addressing the economic crisis and two wars left from the Bush administration. But his voice was strong, his face hopeful and, as if to renew Lincoln's fundamental promise, he said, "I stand here as hopeful as ever that the United States of America will endure."

There were critics who felt all the Lincoln echoes were too self-conscious, even presumptuous. But, as Obama had reminded his advisers in the weeks before the swearing-in ceremony, this was *his* inauguration.

The inaugural festivities had really begun at 11:30 a.m. on Jan. 17, on a blue vintage train car traveling from Philadelphia to Washington, an abridged version of Lincoln's famous journey by rail in 1861. The trip usually took only two hours, but would stretch to seven to factor in the stops for speeches and greeting the mobs of adoring supporters. Michelle Obama, who turned 45 that day, danced in the aisles with Malia, Sasha and some Chicago friends who rode with the family. They picked up Joe and Jill Biden in Wilmington, Del., with Biden making one of the last rides of what had been a daily Amtrak ritual.

"Nah, I don't sweat," Obama replied.

On the day before moving into the world's most venerated house, the Obamas observed a national day of service on the birthday of Dr. Martin Luther King Jr., whose presence had also loomed over the election and the inauguration. As the president-elect painted the walls of a shelter for teenagers in Washington, one of the shelter workers asked if he was sweating.

"Nah, I don't sweat," Obama replied.

The president-elect began his inauguration day with a workout in the Blair House exercise room. Then, at 8:47 a.m. the Obamas left the Blair House for the short drive to St. John's Episcopal Church, just a few blocks away, for a prayer service. It was the first illustration of the bubble of security that had enveloped the Obama family. The short trip required 20 Secret Service agents and a 14-car motorcade, including his new, specially armored Cadillac limousine. Obama wore a dark suit and red tie. Michelle Obama wore a sparkling dress (variously described as golden or the color of lemongrass) and matching coat designed by the Cuban-American designer Isabel Toledo.

Shortly before 10 a.m. and accompanied by the Bidens, the Obamas arrived at the White House. George and Laura Bush met them at the door of their new house. Michelle Obama brought

At the inaugural concert at the Lincoln Memorial, a song from Bruce Springsteen and a gospel choir, and a few words from the guest of honor. January 18, 2009.

IN THIS TEMPLE
AS IN THE HEARTS OF THE PEOPLE
FOR WHOM HE SAVED THE UNION
THE MEMORY OF ABRAHAM LINCOLN
IS ENSHRINED FOREVER

Past and future occupants of the White House meet on its steps. January 20, 2009.

a gift for Laura Bush, a journal and a pen for her to begin her memoirs. About 45 minutes later, the president who was and president who would be entered the limousine that would take them to the Capitol.

As the Obamas and the Bushes headed to the swearing-in, another miracle of democracy was unfolding. Over the next four or five hours, the 93-member White House staff would pack up the belongings of the Bush family and unpack the Obamas', leaving everything belonging to them, down to the girls' socks, neatly folded in drawers. The quick change was accomplished with each new administration, without a single moving man setting foot inside 1600 Pennsylvania Avenue. Michelle's brother, Craig Robinson, had jokingly asked his sister — who chose a prominent Los Angeles-based interior designer, Michael Smith, to help her make the White House a home — how many bathrooms the White House had. (The answer: 34.)

President-elect Obama moments before emerging into the sunlight of his inauguration. January 20, 2009.

Then, for the last time, "Hail to the Chief" was played for George W. Bush.

At the Capitol, the Obama family began arriving. Malia and Sasha smiled and bounced down the steps, a sharp contrast to Vice President Dick Cheney, who had hurt his back packing and had to be wheeled onto the podium in a wheelchair. Then, for the last time, "Hail to the Chief" was played for George W. Bush as he emerged into the sunlight. The brass band seemed to play louder to drown out the boos from the crowd.

DAMON WINTER/NYT

The Rev. Rick Warren, a conservative minister selected by Obama to give the invocation despite protests from liberals and gay activists, told the crowd: "We know today that Dr. King and a great cloud of witnesses are shouting in heaven."

After Biden was sworn in as vice president, Chief Justice John G. Roberts Jr. rose to swear in the president. For a couple of smooth-talking constitutional experts, Roberts and Obama had a hard time getting through the oath of office.

There was, first of all, a false start from the new president, who started to respond before the chief justice had completed the first phrase. He ended up saying the first four words — "I, Barack Hussein Obama" — twice. Then there was an awkward pause after the chief justice prompted Obama with these words: "that I will execute the office of the president to the United States faithfully." The chief justice seemed to say "to" rather than "of," but that was not the main problem. The main problem was that the word "faithfully" had floated upstream in the constitutional text, which actually says this: "that I will faithfully execute the office of the president of the United States."

Obama seemed to realize this, pausing quizzically after saying, "that I will execute —"

The chief justice gave it another go, getting closer but still not quite right: "faithfully the office of president of the United States." This time, he omitted the word "execute."

Aretha Franklin singing "My Country 'Tis of Thee." January 20, 2009.

DAMON WINTER/NYT

PHOTOS: FRED R. CONRAD/NYT
GRAPHIC: FARHANA HOSSAIN AND SERGIO PEÇANHA

Obama then repeated the chief justice's initial error of putting "faithfully" at the end of the phrase. Starting where he had abruptly paused, he said: "the office of the president of the United States faithfully."

The sight of a black man climbing the highest peak electrified people.

It was smooth sailing from there. All of the words in the oath were uttered, along with "so help me God" at the end.

The moment captured the imagination of much of the world as a sea of diverse Americans cheered and cried. Beyond the politics of the occasion, the sight of a black man climbing the highest peak electrified people across racial, generational and partisan lines. In his 18-minute inaugural address, the new president left it to others to explicitly mark the history, making only passing reference to his own barrier-breaking role, that "a man whose father less than 60 years ago might not have been served at a local restaurant can now stand before you to take a most sacred oath."

A thumb's up on the inaugural address from daughter Sasha. January 20, 2009.

"**W**hat was surprising about the speech was how much he dwelled on the choices America faces, rather than the momentousness of his ascension to the presidency."

—*From "Rejecting Bush Era, Reclaiming Values" by David E. Sanger, The New York Times, January 21, 2009*

The somber, muscular tone of the inaugural address surprised some who expected the more soaring rhetoric of the campaign. But this was the speech of a new president completely aware of the crisis confronting him. Even as he began speaking, the Dow Jones average was sinking on another day of huge bank losses.

There were stinging words for Bush, who knew his policies had been widely criticized, yet rarely over the past eight years had to sit in silence listening to a speech about how America had taken a tragic detour. Obama thanked his predecessor, but at several points he bluntly suggested that Bush had left things in a shambles.

The new president implicitly criticized Bush when he talked of "how the ways we use energy strengthen our adversaries and threaten our planet," and noted that the Cold War was won "not just with missiles and tanks," but by leaders who understood "that our power alone cannot protect us, nor does it entitle us to do as we please." It grows instead, he said, "through its prudent use."

It was a message much of the world was waiting to hear. But

it was matched with a warning to America's enemies, especially terrorists and terror-sponsoring nations, that "you cannot outlast us, and we will defeat you."

Obama leavened the celebration with a sober assessment of the state of the economy, noting the spate of home foreclosures, shuttered businesses, lost jobs, costly health care, failing schools, energy dependence and the threat of climate change.

"Less measurable but no less profound is a sapping of confidence across our land, a nagging fear that America's decline is inevitable, that the next generation must lower its sights," he said. "Today, I say to you that the challenges we face are real. They are serious and they are many. They will not be met easily or in a short span of time. But know this, America: They will be met."

On The Times's Web site, a panel of former presidential speechwriters assessed the address. William Safire, a former Times columnist and speechwriter for President Richard Nixon, wrote, "Our 44th president's Inaugural Address was solid, respectable, uplifting, suitably short, superbly delivered, but — in light of the

"Yet not since 1933, when Franklin D. Roosevelt called for a 'restoration' of American ethics and 'action, and action now' as Herbert Hoover sat and seethed, has a new president so publicly rejected the essence of his predecessor's path."

—From "Rejecting Bush Era, Reclaiming Values" by David E. Sanger, The New York Times, January 21, 2009

INAUGURAL ADDRESS

JANUARY 20, 2009

My fellow citizens:

I stand here today humbled by the task before us, grateful for the trust you have bestowed, mindful of the sacrifices borne by our ancestors. I thank President Bush for his service to our nation, as well as the generosity and cooperation he has shown throughout this transition.

Forty-four Americans have now taken the presidential oath. The words have been spoken during rising tides of prosperity and the still waters of peace. Yet, every so often the oath is taken amidst gathering clouds and raging storms. At these moments, America has carried on not simply because of the skill or vision of those in high office, but because we the people have remained faithful to the ideals of our forbearers, and true to our founding documents.

So it has been. So it must be with this generation of Americans.

That we are in the midst of crisis is now well understood. Our nation is at war against a far-reaching network of violence and hatred. Our economy is badly weakened, a consequence of greed and irresponsibility on the part of some, but also our collective failure to make hard choices and prepare the nation for a new age. Homes have been lost, jobs shed, businesses shuttered. Our health care is too costly, our schools fail too

DAMON WINTER / NYT

many and each day brings further evidence that the ways we use energy strengthen our adversaries and threaten our planet.

These are the indicators of crisis, subject to data and statistics. Less measurable, but no less profound, is a sapping of confidence across our land — a nagging fear that America's decline is inevitable, that the next generation must lower its sights.

Today I say to you that the challenges we face are real, they are serious and they are many. They will not be met easily or in a short span of time. But know this, America: They will be met.

On this day, we gather because we have chosen hope over fear, unity of purpose over conflict and discord.

On this day, we come to proclaim an end to the petty grievances and false promises, the recriminations and worn-out dogmas that for far too long have strangled our politics.

We remain a young nation, but in the words of Scripture, the time has come to set aside childish things. The time has come to reaffirm our enduring spirit; to choose our better history; to carry forward that precious gift, that noble idea, passed on from generation to generation: the God-given promise that all are equal, all are free and all deserve a chance to pursue their full measure of happiness.

In reaffirming the greatness of our nation, we understand that greatness is never a given. It must be earned. Our journey has never been one of short cuts or settling for less. It has not been the path for the faint-hearted — for those who prefer leisure over work, or seek only the pleasures of riches and fame. Rather, it has been the risk-takers, the doers, the makers of things — some celebrated but more often men and women obscure in their labor — who have carried us up the long, rugged path towards prosperity and freedom.

For us, they packed up their few worldly possessions and traveled across oceans in search of a new life.

For us, they toiled in sweatshops and settled the West; endured the lash of the whip and plowed the hard earth.

For us, they fought and died, in places like Concord and Gettysburg, Normandy and Khe Sanh.

Time and again these men and women struggled and sacrificed and worked til their hands were raw so that we might live a better life. They saw America as bigger than the sum of our individual ambitions; greater than all the differences of birth or wealth or faction.

This is the journey we continue today. We remain the most prosperous, powerful nation on Earth. Our workers are no less productive than when this crisis began. Our minds are no less inventive, our goods and services no less needed than they were last week or last month or last year. Our capacity remains undiminished. But our time of standing pat, of protecting narrow interests and putting off unpleasant decisions — that time has surely passed. Starting today, we must pick ourselves up, dust ourselves off and begin again the work of remaking America.

For everywhere we look, there is work to be done. The state of the economy calls for action, bold and swift, and we will act — not only to create new jobs, but to lay a new foundation for growth. We will build the roads and bridges, the electric grids and digital lines that feed our commerce and bind us together. We will restore science to its rightful place and wield technology's wonders to raise health care's quality and lower its cost. We will harness the sun and the winds and the soil to fuel our cars and run our factories. And we will transform our schools and colleges and universities to meet the demands of a new age. All this we can do. And all this we will do.

Now, there are some who question the scale of our ambitions — who suggest that our system cannot tolerate too many big plans. Their memories are short, for they have forgotten what this country has already done, what free men and women can achieve when imagination is joined to common purpose, and necessity to courage.

What the cynics fail to understand is that the ground has shifted beneath them — that the stale political arguments that have consumed us for so long no longer apply. The question we ask today is not whether our government is too big or too small, but whether it works — whether it helps families find jobs at a decent wage, care they can afford, a retirement that is dignified. Where the answer is yes, we intend to move forward. Where the answer is no, programs will end. And those of us who manage the public's dollars will be held to account — to spend wisely, reform bad habits and do our business in the light of day — because only then can we restore the vital trust between a people and their government.

Nor is the question before us whether the market is a force for good or ill. Its power to generate wealth and expand freedom is unmatched, but this crisis has reminded us that without a watchful eye, the market can spin out of control — and that a nation cannot prosper long when it favors only the prosperous. The success of our economy has always depended not just on the size of our Gross Domestic Product, but on the reach of our prosperity; on our ability to extend opportunity to every willing heart — not out of charity, but because it is the surest route to our common good.

As for our common defense, we reject as false the choice between our safety and our ideals. Our founding fathers, faced with perils we can scarcely imagine, drafted a charter to assure the rule of law and the rights of man, a charter expanded by the blood of generations. Those ideals still light the world, and we will not give them up for expedience's sake. And so to all other peoples and governments who are watching today, from the grandest capitals to the small village where my father was born: know that America is a friend of each nation and every man, woman and child who seeks a future of peace and dignity, and that we are ready to lead once more.

Recall that earlier generations faced down fascism and communism not just with missiles and tanks, but with sturdy alliances and enduring convictions. They understood that our power alone cannot protect us, nor does it entitle us to do as we please. Instead, they knew that our power grows through its prudent use; our security emanates from the justness of our cause, the force of our example, the tempering qualities of humility and restraint.

We are the keepers of this legacy. Guided by these principles once more, we can meet those new threats that demand even greater effort — even greater cooperation and understanding between nations. We will begin to responsibly leave Iraq to its people and forge a hard-earned peace in Afghanistan. With old friends and former foes, we will work tirelessly to lessen the nuclear threat, and roll back the specter of a warming planet. We will not apologize for our way of life, nor will we waver in its defense, and for those who seek to advance their aims by inducing terror and slaughtering innocents, we say to you now that our spirit is stronger and cannot be broken; you cannot outlast us, and we will defeat you.

For we know that our patchwork heritage is a strength, not a weakness. We are a nation of Christians and Muslims, Jews and Hindus — and non-believers. We are shaped by every language and culture, drawn from every end of this Earth; and because we have tasted the bitter swill of civil war and segregation and emerged from that dark chapter stronger and more united, we cannot help but believe that the old hatreds shall someday pass; that the lines of tribe shall soon dissolve; that as the world grows smaller, our common humanity shall reveal itself; and that America must play its role in ushering in a new era of peace.

To the Muslim world, we seek a new way forward, based on mutual interest and mutual respect. To those leaders around the globe who seek to sow conflict, or blame their society's ills on the West — know that your people will judge you on what you can build, not what you destroy. To those who cling to power through corruption and deceit and the silencing of dissent, know that you are on the wrong side of history, but that we will extend a hand if you are willing to unclench your fist.

To the people of poor nations, we pledge to work alongside you to make your farms flourish and let clean waters flow; to nourish starved bodies and feed hungry minds. And to those nations like ours that enjoy relative plenty, we say we can no longer afford indifference to suffering outside our borders; nor can we consume the world's resources without regard to effect. For the world has changed, and we must change with it.

As we consider the road that unfolds before us, we remember with humble gratitude those brave Americans who, at this very hour, patrol far-off deserts and distant mountains. They have something to tell us, just as the fallen heroes who lie in Arlington whisper through the ages. We honor them not only because they are guardians of our liberty, but because they embody the spirit of service, a willingness to find meaning in something greater than themselves. And yet, at this moment — a moment that will define a generation — it is precisely this spirit that must inhabit us all.

For as much as government can do and must do, it is ultimately the faith and determination of the American people upon which this nation relies. It is the kindness to take in a stranger when the levees break, the selflessness of workers who would rather cut their hours than see a friend lose their job, which sees us through our darkest hours. It is the firefighter's courage to storm a stairway filled with smoke, but also a parent's willingness to nurture a child, that finally decides our fate.

Our challenges may be new. The instruments with which we meet them may be new. But those values upon which our success depends — hard work and honesty, courage and fair play, tolerance and curiosity, loyalty and patriotism — these things are old. These things are true. They have been the quiet force of progress throughout our history. What is demanded, then, is a return to these truths. What is required of us now is a new era of responsibility — a recognition, on the part of every American, that we have duties to ourselves, our nation and the world, duties that we do not grudgingly accept but rather seize gladly, firm in the knowledge that there is nothing so satisfying to the spirit, so defining of our character, than giving our all to a difficult task.

This is the price and the promise of citizenship.

This is the source of our confidence — the knowledge that God calls on us to shape an uncertain destiny.

This is the meaning of our liberty and our creed — why men and women and children of every race and every faith can join in celebration across this magnificent mall, and why a man whose father less than 60 years ago might not have been served at a local restaurant can now stand before you to take a most sacred oath.

So let us mark this day with remembrance of who we are and how far we have traveled. In the year of America's birth, in the coldest of months, a small band of patriots huddled by dying campfires on the shores of an icy river. The capital was abandoned. The enemy was advancing. The snow was stained with blood. At a moment when the outcome of our revolution was most in doubt, the father of our nation ordered these words be read to the people:

"Let it be told to the future world . . . that in the depth of winter, when nothing but hope and virtue could survive . . . that the city and the country, alarmed at one common danger, came forth to meet it."

America, in the face of our common dangers, in this winter of our hardship, let us remember these timeless words. With hope and virtue, let us brave once more the icy currents, and endure what storms may come. Let it be said by our children's children that when we were tested we refused to let this journey end, that we did not turn back nor did we falter; and with eyes fixed on the horizon and God's grace upon us, we carried forth that great gift of freedom and delivered it safely to future generations.

Thank you, God bless you and God bless the United States of America. ◆

In reaffirming the greatness of our nation, we understand that greatness is never a given. It must be earned.

POOL PHOTO BY MOLLY RILEY

Post-inaugural duties included seeing off the Bushes and signing a proclamation amid members of the Joint Congressional Committee on inaugural ceremonies. January 20, 2009.

towering expectations whipped up that his speech might belong in the company of those by Lincoln, F.D.R. and Kennedy — fell short of the anticipated immortality."

Sasha Obama's appraisal was more succinct: "That was a pretty good speech, Dad."

Obama was visibly moved when, 146 years after the Emancipation Proclamation, 108 years after the first black man dined in the mansion with a president and 45 years after Martin Luther King Jr. declared his dream of equality, the Rev. Joseph E. Lowery, one of the towering figures of the civil rights movement, gave the benediction and preached for "inclusion, not exclusion, tolerance, not intolerance."

The last ritual of the inaugural program was seeing off the Bushes for their trip home to Texas. Bush hugged Obama, then headed out through the Rotunda. "Come on, Laura, we're going home," he was overheard telling the former first lady.

Oath Is Administered Once Again
Jeff Zeleny

President Obama was re-administered the oath of office on Wednesday evening by Chief Justice John G. Roberts Jr., one day after the two men stumbled over each other's words during the inauguration.

The president and the chief justice stood in the Map Room of the White House at 7:35 p.m. as they took a second run at the constitutional oath. A handful of advisers watched the proceeding, which lasted about 25 seconds.

"Are you ready to take the oath?" Mr. Roberts said.

"I am," Mr. Obama replied. "And we're going to do it very slowly."

Gregory Craig, the White House counsel, said he believes the oath was "administered effectively and that the president was sworn in appropriately." But out of caution and to ward off any speculation that he wasn't properly sworn in, aides decided on Wednesday afternoon to give the oath another try.

"The oath appears in the Constitution itself," Mr. Craig said in a statement. "And out of an abundance of caution, because there was one word out of sequence, Chief Justice Roberts administered the oath a second time."

At the swearing-in ceremony on Tuesday, Mr. Roberts juxtaposed a word in the oath when he said, "That I will execute the office of president to the United States faithfully." The word "faithfully" was misplaced.

As set out in the Constitution, this is what Mr. Obama should have said:

I do solemnly swear (or affirm) that I will faithfully execute the Office of the President of the United States, and will to the best of my ability, preserve, protect and defend the Constitution of the United States. (Like most of his predecessors, Mr. Obama swore, rather than affirmed, and like some past presidents he appended "so help me God" to the standard text.)

During a luncheon after the inauguration ceremony, Mr. Roberts could be seen on camera telling the president that the mistake was "my fault." So he agreed to travel to the White House on Wednesday evening for a ceremony that was not announced until it was over.

The New York Times, January 21, 2009

The most visible signs of the end of Bush's power were the new White House's plans to close the detention center at Guantánamo Bay, Cuba, and the reversal of Bush's restrictions on funding for groups that promote abortion or condom use. One of President Obama's first acts in office was to issue a 120-day stay for all proceedings involving Guantánamo detainees.

Maureen Dowd captured the moment in her column. "It was like a catharsis in Greek drama, with the antagonist plucked out of the scene into the sky, and the protagonist dropping into the scene to magically fix all the problems. Except Barack Obama's somber mien and restrained oratory conveyed that he's no divinity and there will be no easy resolution to this plot. I grew up here, and it was the first time I've ever seen the city wholly, happily integrated, with a mood redolent of New York in the weeks after 9/11."

Sasha Obama's appraisal was more succinct: "That was a pretty good speech, Dad."

The joyful spirit of the day was marred by the hospitalization of Senator Edward M. Kennedy, the liberal icon whose endorsement helped propel Obama to the Democratic nomination. Kennedy, who had been fighting a malignant brain tumor, collapsed in convulsions during a Capitol luncheon after the ceremony and was wheeled out on a stretcher. Later it was announced that the senator was talking and not in immediate danger. He went home the next day.

On the streets of Washington, strangers hugged one another. Many could no longer feel their feet from standing in the cold, but there was dancing anyway. "There was something very private and almost personal about being here and then hearing that voice," said Tiajuana Lee, a 42-year-old schoolteacher who traveled with her family from Kentwood, La.

Across the country and around the world, there were equally jubilant displays. In Birmingham, Ala., Robbie Revis Smith, 73, twice jailed in the 1960s for her part in the civil rights struggle, had wanted to make the trip to Washington but a bad back made it almost impossible for her to stand. So she sat in a darkened concert hall clapping with the Rev. Fred L. Shuttlesworth, the 86-year-old survivor of bombings and beatings, now confined

The Obamas walked part of the parade route. January 20, 2009.

Some of the surviving Tuskegee Airmen, the black-only World War II fighting force, came to Washington, D.C. January 20, 2009.

OZIER MUHAMMAD/NYT

Soldiers celebrate the inauguration, Kabul, Afghanistan. January 20, 2009.

MUSADEQ SADEQ/AP

to a wheelchair. In Kisumu, Kenya, where Obama's father was born, people stood atop their bicycles to watch the inaugural party celebrating the son of their former countryman becoming the new American president. Iraqis gathered in cafes in Baghdad to watch the televised coverage, while American soldiers exchanged high fives at a base in Kabul.

> *There was evidence that, as enthusiastic as the American public was about the change in power, there were no expectations of quick fixes.*

Some worried that expectations were too high. "Obviously, there is a risk that we will expect too much of this president — that we will learn that however talented he is, he isn't a global miracle worker," said Christopher Patten, a former European commissioner for foreign affairs and chancellor of Oxford.

There was evidence that, as enthusiastic as the American public was about the change in power, there were no expectations of quick fixes. The cascade of grim economic news, combined with the calculatedly sober tone Obama adopted, provided something of a cushion for him. So did opinion polls showing him with the strongest approval ratings of any recent new president.

Obama's advisers — who stressed that fixing the economy and enacting huge initiatives, like overhauling the nation's health care and energy policies, were not going to happen quickly — wished to avoid being nailed down on any specific timetables. "I just don't know," the new senior White House adviser David Axelrod said. "I think right now people are inclined to give us some time. By time I mean more than months. People understand that it's going to take years."

A New York Times/CBS News Poll conducted just before the inauguration offered at least some guidance for the Obama expectations clock. Most respondents said they thought it would take two years or more to deliver on campaign promises to improve the economy, expand health care coverage and end the war in Iraq.

A crowd gathered in Kisumu, Kenya, for musical performances in honor of the inauguration. January 20, 2009.

Excitement at the Youth Ball as the Obamas pass by. January 20, 2009.

But for one day the problems could wait. Along the inaugural parade route, tens of thousands jockeyed to catch a glimpse of the new president. Despite the extremely tight security and the worried looks of their Secret Service detail, the Obamas twice emerged from their car to walk the parade route, holding hands and beaming at their adoring, shrieking fans. One group of marchers had a special place in the new president's heart: the band from the Punahou School from Hawaii.

> *At one of their stops, he asked the crowd, "First of all, how good-looking is my wife?"*

After the parade, the first couple briefly darted into the White House to freshen up and did not return again until 7 p.m., to quickly change into formal attire. While Malia and Sasha watched movies in their new home, their parents emerged for their big night out, he in a new tuxedo and white bow tie, she in a gown made of ivory silk chiffon, embellished with organza and Swarovski crystal rhinestones and silver thread embroidery. It was custom-designed and made exclusively for Michelle Obama by Jason Wu, a 26-year-old New York designer.

The Obamas attended 10 of the inaugural balls, first to the D.C. Neighborhood Inaugural Ball, a symbolic choice given the first couple's pledge to deeply involve themselves in the fabric of the city rather than living their lives in the predominantly white Oz of the Washington political elite. For their first dance, Beyoncé sang "At Last." At the Commander in Chief Ball, the new president chatted via satellite with a military team from Illinois serving in Afghanistan. At one of their stops, he asked the crowd, "First of all, how good-looking is my wife?"

His next date, the one with the Oval Office, would arrive in a few hours. ♦

Dancing at the Commander in Chief Ball. January 20, 2009.

Commentary

Bring On the Puppy and the Rookie

MAUREEN DOWD

I walked over to the White House Tuesday night and leaned against the fence. How can such a lovely house make so many of its inhabitants nuts?

There was no U-Haul in the driveway. I don't know if W. was inside talking to the portraits on the wall. Or if the portraits can vanish from their frames, as at Hogwarts Academy, to escape if W. is pestering them about his legacy.

The Obama girls, with their oodles of charm, will soon be moving in with their goldendoodle or some other fetching puppy, and they seem like the kind of kids who could have fun there, prowling around with their history-loving father.

I had been amazed during the campaign — not by the covert racism about Barack Obama and not by Hillary Clinton's subtext when she insisted to superdelegates: "He can't win."

But I had been astonished by the overt willingness of some people who didn't mind being quoted by name in The New York Times saying vile stuff, that a President Obama would turn the Rose Garden into a watermelon patch, that he'd have barbeques on the front lawn, that he'd make the White House the Black House.

Actually, the elegant and disciplined Obama, who is not descended from the central African-American experience but who has nonetheless embraced it and been embraced by it, has the chance to make the White House pristine again.

I grew up here, and I love all the monuments filled with the capital's ghosts. I hate the thought that terrorists might target them again.

But the monuments have lost their luminescence in recent years.

> Obama may be in over his head. Or he may be heading for his own monument one day.

How could the White House be classy when the Clintons were turning it into Motel 1600 for fund-raising, when Bill Clinton was using it for trysts with an intern and when he plunked a seven-seat hot tub with two Moto-Massager jets on the lawn?

How could the White House be inspiring when W. and Cheney were inside making torture and domestic spying legal, fooling Americans by cooking up warped evidence for war and scheming how to further enrich their buddies in the oil and gas industry?

How could the Lincoln Memorial — "With malice toward none; with charity for all" — be as moving if the black neighborhoods of a charming American city were left to drown while the president mountain-biked?

How can the National Archives, home of the Constitution, be as momentous if the president and vice president spend their days redacting the Constitution?

How can the black marble V of the Vietnam Memorial have power when those in power repeat the mistake of Vietnam?

How can the Capitol, where my dad proudly worked for so many years, hold its allure when the occupants have spent their days — and years — bickering and scoring petty political points instead of stopping White House chicanery and taking on risky big issues?

How can the F.D.R. Memorial along the Tidal Basin be an uplifting trip to the past when the bronze statue of five stooped men in a bread line and the words of F.D.R.'s second inaugural — "I see one-third of a nation ill-housed, ill-clad and ill-nourished" — evokes the depressing present?

Obama may be in over his head. Or he may be heading for his own monument one day.

His somber speech in the dark Chicago night was stark

and simple and showed that he sees what he's up against. There was a heaviness in his demeanor, as if he already had taken on the isolation and "splendid misery," as Jefferson called it, of the office he'd won only moments before. Americans all over the place were jumping for joy, including the block I had been on in front of the White House, where they were singing: "Na, na, na, na. Hey, hey, hey. Goodbye."

In the midst of such a phenomenal, fizzy victory overcoming so many doubts and crazy attacks and even his own middle name, Obama stood alone.

He rejected the Democratic kumbaya moment of having your broad coalition on stage with you, as he talked about how everyone would have to pull together and "resist the temptation to fall back on the same partisanship and pettiness and immaturity that has poisoned our politics for so long."

He professed "humility," but we'd heard that before from W., and look what happened there.

Promising to also be president for those who opposed him, Obama quoted Lincoln, his political idol and the man who ended slavery: "We are not enemies, but friends — though passion may have strained it must not break our bonds of affection."

There have been many awful mistakes made in this country. But now we have another chance.

As we start fresh with a constitutional law professor and senator from the Land of Lincoln, the Lincoln Memorial might be getting its gleam back.

I may have to celebrate by going over there and climbing up into Abe's lap.

It's a $50 fine. But it'd be worth it. ♦

Originally published in The New York Times, November 6, 2008

NOMA BAR

KARA WALKER

Let Reconstruction Begin

THOMAS L. FRIEDMAN

And so it came to pass that on Nov. 4, 2008, shortly after 11 p.m. Eastern time, the American Civil War ended, as a black man — Barack Hussein Obama — won enough electoral votes to become president of the United States.

A civil war that, in many ways, began at Bull Run, Va., on July 21, 1861, ended 147 years later via a ballot box in the very same state. For nothing more symbolically illustrated the final chapter than the fact that the Commonwealth of Virginia — the state that once exalted slavery and whose secession from the Union in 1861 gave the Confederacy both strategic weight and its commanding general — voted Democratic, thus assuring that Barack Obama would become the 44th president of the United States.

Despite a century of civil rights legislation, judicial interventions and social activism — despite Brown v. Board of Education, Martin Luther King's I-have-a-dream crusade and the 1964 Civil Rights Act — one could not say that the Civil War was truly over until that moment when America's white majority actually elected an African-American as president. That is what happened in this election and that is why in its wake we are a different country, a better country.

The struggle for equal rights is far from over, but we start afresh now from a whole new baseline. Let every child and every citizen and every new immigrant know that from this day forward everything really is possible in America.

How did Obama pull it off? To be sure, it probably took a once-in-a-century economic crisis to get enough white people

> One really could not say that the Civil War was truly over until that moment when America's white majority actually elected an African-American as president.

to vote for a black man. And to be sure, Obama's better organization, calm manner, mellifluous speaking style and unthreatening message of "change" all served him well. But there also may have been something that countered the supposed "Bradley effect" — white voters telling pollsters they'd vote for Obama but then voting for the white guy. Call it the Buffett effect, white conservatives telling the guys in the men's grill at the local country club that they were voting for John McCain, but then quietly going into the booth and voting for Obama, even though they knew it could mean higher taxes.

Why? Some did it because they sensed how inspired and hopeful their kids were about an Obama presidency, and they not only didn't want to dash those hopes, they secretly wanted to share them. Others intuitively embraced Warren Buffett's view that if you are rich and successful today, it is first and foremost because you were lucky enough to be born in America at this time — and never forget that. So, that theory goes, we need to get back to fixing our country — we need a president who can unify us for nation-building at home. It was that gnawing, often unarticulated, intuition that propelled Obama's victory more than anything else.

And now the question going forward: Barack Obama will always be our first black president, but can he be one of our great presidents? He is going to have his chance because our greatest presidents are those who assumed the office at some of our darkest hours and at the bottom of some of our deepest holes.

"Taking office at a time of crisis doesn't guarantee greatness, but it can be an occasion for it," argued the Harvard University political philosopher Michael Sandel. "That was certainly the case with Lincoln, F.D.R. and Truman." Part of F.D.R.'s greatness, though, "was that he gradually wove a new governing political philosophy — the New Deal — out of the rubble and political disarray of the economic depression he inherited." Obama will need to do the same, but these things take time — and courage.

To me, the greatest irony of his election is that Obama spent so much time and energy trying to prove that he was not a radical, when his time in office is likely to demand more radical decisions than any post-Franklin D. Roosevelt president. My gut tells me that the biggest challenge Obama will face is to be as radical as the moment that brought him to power. His election was a radical departure from our past; the economic crisis in which he takes power is a radical departure from what has been the norm for nearly a century; the way out of this crisis will require radical economic policies, the likes of which were never really discussed in the campaign or contemplated since the Great Depression.

"F.D.R. did not run on the New Deal in 1932," said Sandel. "He ran on balancing the budget. Like Obama, he did not take office with a clearly articulated governing philosophy. He arrived with a confident, activist spirit and experimented. Not until 1936 did we have a presidential campaign about the New Deal. What Obama's equivalent will be, even he doesn't know. It will emerge as he grapples with the economy, energy and America's role in the world. These challenges are so great that he will only succeed if he is able to articulate a new politics of the common good."

Bush & Co. did not believe that government could be an instrument of the common good. They neutered their cabinet secretaries and appointed hacks to big jobs. For them, pursuit of the common good was all about pursuit of individual self-interest. Voters rebelled against that. But there was also a rebellion against a traditional Democratic version of the common good — that it is simply the sum of all interest groups clamoring for their share.

"In this election, the American public rejected these narrow notions of the common good," argued Sandel. "Most people now accept that unfettered markets don't serve the public good." He added, "Obama will have to reinvent government as an instrument of the common good — to regulate markets, to protect citizens against the risks of unemployment and ill health, to invest in energy independence."

But a new politics of the common good can't be only about government and markets. "It must also be about a new patriotism — about what it means to be a citizen," said Sandel. "This is the deepest chord Obama's campaign evoked. The biggest applause line in his stump speech was the one that said every American will have a chance to go to college provided he or she performs a period of national service — in the military, in the Peace Corps or in the community. Obama's campaign tapped a dormant civic idealism, a hunger among Americans to serve a cause greater than themselves, a yearning to be citizens again."

None of this will be easy.

Will Obama have the courage of our crisis? Will he be willing to contemplate financial rescue packages with more zeros than any president has ever signed onto? Will he be willing to shut down financial institutions and companies that cannot be bailed out so that the markets can clear and start over — even if it sends unemployment temporarily into the stratosphere? We will find out soon enough.

On paper, at least, he would seem to be the ideal president for this time — a time that will require a great unifier, with a cool head and calming manner, to hold the country together through the wrenching restructuring that will be required to steady our Republic. I remain hopeful. The times make the man and the Obama raw material seems to be very solid and workable.

What I am more certain of, though, is this: of all the changes that will be ushered in by an Obama presidency, breaking with our racial past may turn out to be the least of them. There is just so much work to be done, so many radical departures to set in motion. The Civil War is over. Let Reconstruction begin. ◆

> He would seem to be the ideal president for this time — a time that will require a great unifier, with a cool head and calming manner, to hold the country together through the wrenching restructuring that will be required to steady our Republic.

ELIZABETH PEYTON